Guide to Qualitative Research in Parliaments

Valentine Berthet · Barbara Gaweda ·
Johanna Kantola · Cherry Miller ·
Petra Ahrens · Anna Elomäki

Guide to Qualitative Research in Parliaments

Experiences and Practices

Valentine Berthet 🆔
Centre for European Studies
University of Helsinki
Helsinki, Finland

Johanna Kantola 🆔
Centre for European Studies
University of Helsinki
Helsinki, Finland

Petra Ahrens 🆔
The Faculty of Social Sciences
Tampere University
Tampere, Finland

Barbara Gaweda 🆔
Centre for European Studies
University of Helsinki
Helsinki, Finland

Cherry Miller 🆔
British and Comparative Politics
University of Glasgow
Glasgow, UK

Anna Elomäki 🆔
The Faculty of Social Sciences
Tampere University
Tampere, Finland

ISBN 978-3-031-39807-0   ISBN 978-3-031-39808-7   (eBook)
https://doi.org/10.1007/978-3-031-39808-7

Cover illustration: © Melisa Hasan

This Palgrave Macmillan imprint is published by the registered company Springer Nature Switzerland AG
The registered company address is: Gewerbestrasse 11, 6330 Cham, Switzerland

Acknowledgements

This book and the research it is based upon were made possible thanks to the funding received from the European Research Council (ERC) under the European Union's Horizon 2020 research and innovation programme grant number 771676. We are deeply indebted to the members of our Academic Expert Board for suggesting the idea of such a book and for inspiring us to share our experiences with others.

This research would not have been so rich and rewarding without the interviewees and contacts in the European Parliament that generously granted us access to the parliamentary premises and dedicated their time to answer our questions. Thank you for sharing your time and insights. Moreover, we would like to thank our two wonderful research assistants, Säde Kunnas and Ansa Ahola at the University of Helsinki. The completion of this book would not have been possible without your help and support. Finally, a big thank you to Fraser King, for your sense of humour and patience in proof-reading the messy writing of six different authors.

In Helsinki, Glasgow and Berlin

May 2023

Valentine Berthet
Barbara Gaweda
Johanna Kantola
Cherry Miller
Petra Ahrens
Anna Elomäki

CONTENTS

Abbreviations

AfD	Alternative für Deutschland (Alternative for Germany)
ALDE	Alliance of Liberals and Democrats for Europe
APA	Accredited Parliamentary Assistant
ECON	Economic and Monetary Affairs Committee
ECR	European Conservatives and Reformists
EFDD	Europe of Freedom and Direct Democracy
EMPL	Employment and Social Affairs Committee
ENF	Europe of Nations and Freedom
EP	European Parliament
EPP	The Group of the European People's Party/The European People's Party
EU	European Union
FEMM	European Parliament's Committee on Women's Rights and Gender Equality
GDPR	General Data Protection Regulation
Greens/EFA	Greens–European Free Alliance
GUE/NGL	The Left in the European Parliament (previously European United Left/Nordic Green Left)
ID	Identity & Democracy
LGBTIQ	Lesbian, Gay, Bisexual, Trans, Intersex and Queer
LIBE	European Parliament's Committee on Civil Liberties, Justice and Home Affairs
MEP	Member of the European Parliament
MP	Member of Parliament
PG	Political Group
Renew	Renew Europe

S&D	Progressive Alliance of Socialists and Democrats
SG	Secretary General
UK	United Kingdom
VPN	Virtual Private Network

LIST OF FIGURES

LIST OF TABLES

LIST OF BOXES

Introduction to a Practical Guide on Conducting Qualitative Research in Parliaments

Abstract The first chapter introduces the focus and goals of the volume, by explaining its hands-on approach to research and outlining its qualitative interpretive methodological nature. The aim is to provide concrete tips on how to overcome fieldwork obstacles as well as serve as invaluable background or context material for anyone who aims to research the European Parliament, with useful pointers for anyone who wants to work on political institutions and do qualitative interviews. Attention is drawn to the utility of the volume for researchers who examine highly divisive subjects like equality policies or the ways of dealing with radical-right actors in qualitative research when holding opposing views. Instead of merely analysing research results, the book is an honest account of how they were obtained.

Keywords EUGenDem project · Hands-on guide · Political institutions · Gendered perspectives · Intersectional perspectives

© The Author(s) 2023
V. Berthet et al., *Guide to Qualitative Research in Parliaments*,
https://doi.org/10.1007/978-3-031-39808-7_1

INTRODUCTION

How is a large-scale qualitative dataset, comprised of interview, ethnographic and document data, gathered from parliaments? In what ways are raw data managed in terms of storing and coding? What methods are employed to interpret and make sense of coded data? More significantly, how are qualitative data that have been collectively gathered and coded, transformed into findings for single and co-authored articles?

This volume addresses these questions in the form of a concise and hands-on guide about doing qualitative research in parliaments, exploring practical achievements and drawbacks that are relevant to academics and students alike. We account for the step-by-step process of qualitative research in parliaments, offering a reflexive and analytical perspective that moves beyond a textbook or theory-only format. As a companion piece to qualitative research in parliaments, we also 'accompany' and support researchers in the field who may feel they are struggling or have become lost. Woven throughout the individual chapters, the book provides meaningful insights into the methodological and normative concerns our research process faced. To this end, we include many examples and illustrative boxes presenting our research diaries, post-interview notes and coding examples to illustrate the distinct processes and stages in our research and to demonstrate how our thinking developed leading to the final research output.

This approach has enabled us to provide a more transparent perspective on the research process through the views of insiders, as two distinctive stages of data gathering (Chapters 3 and 4) and data analysis (Chapters 5 and 6) unfold to form a coherent whole. In doing so, the insights account for different positionalities, epistemological commitments and research interests, thus providing useful hints for anyone who wants to study and research formal political institutions like parliaments, using qualitative methods. Throughout the volume, the experiences we describe, provide invaluable ideas for strategies and practices that researchers can adopt to overcome the typical obstacles that qualitative researchers might face. For instance, we detail in Chapter 4 the strategies we employed for recruiting interview participants and for preparing to conduct an interview; and in Chapter 5, we provide a number of core points for successful collaborative coding.

In lieu of analysing and outlining research findings specifically, we focus on how those outputs were obtained. To this end, the European Parliament (EP) provided the setting and context between 2018 and 2022, for gathering a large and significant volume of interviews, ethnographic fieldnotes and documents. Empirically, the volume stands as an important background read for anyone aiming to study the European Parliament regardless of the methodology. We provide multiple insights on the specificities of the European Parliament including its monthly calendar, the opportunities and obstacles provided by the Strasbourg sessions and the challenges of the multilingual and multi-language settings. The book also provides extensive insights into studying political institutions like parliaments in general. In this sense, the book makes general observations on the functioning of parliamentary work and presents advice based on experiences, practices and strategies for any researcher wanting to apply qualitative methods and tools to the study of parliaments.

The Research Project and Findings

This volume provides an account of a major scientific research project conducted on the political groups of the European Parliament, the insights from which will have wider and more general applications in academia. The EUGenDem project on *'Gender, party politics and democracy in Europe: a study of the European Parliament's party groups'* was a European Research Council Consolidator Grant funded scientific project that provided a systematic analysis of the gendered policies and practices of the political groups in the European Parliament. Whilst most research on the political groups has been quantitative, EUGenDem research led to over 70 scientific publications based on qualitative methods and methodologies. We have written about the positionality and reflexivity of our research team elsewhere (Gaweda et al., 2022; Kantola et al., 2023) suffice it to say our approach was normatively feminist and epistemologically constructivist, giving it a distinct piquancy from most of the extant research in the field.

Our motivation for this volume was derived from the keen interest of colleagues, anonymous reviewers as well as the members of our project scientific board, to disclose and elaborate on conducting impactful qualitative research (Ahrens et al., 2022; Kantola et al., 2023), and to detail our processes of data gathering and data analysis. Following the ideals of open, accessible and transparent research, we want to ensure that key qualitative research strategies are available to, and reusable by, other researchers. In addition, there is a necessity to both invigorate and disturb extant academic debates on the use and relevance of qualitative research methods in Political Science from a multidisciplinary perspective. Of notable importance in this respect, is the particularity of our collective approach to conducting qualitative research. In the book, we explain in greater detail the extent to which this constituted a significant advantage, and how we resolved, or managed, the additional complexities it brought about.

The retrospective and reflexive look at our research field itself also yields insights. Reflecting on the qualitative nature of the research project, we examine the ways in which divisive questions were often asked, political controversies were researched and how we confronted and dealt with equality practices, issues of gender equality, racism and radical-right populists. Box 1.1 (below) highlights some examples from our interview and ethnographic fieldwork that best describe such moments. Such highly divisive subjects, like the study of equality policies and the role of radical-right populist parties in parliament, fall within the scope of our guide. Qualitative research from a gendered perspective demonstrates how actors are positioned in multiple contexts and within variant identities, which demands that an intersectional lens must be considered more systematically, and in-depth, at the beginning of a project.

We did not shy away from interviewing right-wing actors and concomitantly did not focus only on 'feminist critical friends' (Chappell, 2020; Chappell & Mackay, 2021). Instead, we emphasised the importance of approaching interviews with right-wing actors with a critical and reflexive mindset, whilst being mindful of the potential for power imbalances to arise. Right-wing participants often used gendered language or stereotypes that were dismissive or undermining of our normative stances and arguments; they also sometimes questioned the legitimacy of our qualifications or expertise. For instance, Kantola et al. (2023) illustrated how one participant explicitly asked the interviewer: 'I think it's just one of these throwaway terms that's been invented by (…), in the same way that racism is a made-up term. Do you know what racism means? You're a doctor so obviously you should know, right?' (EFDD MEP M 290119_4). In another example, a male MEP from the radical-right and a member of the Eurosceptic group of the European Conservatives and Reformists

(ECR) discussed the family in a public seminar. Claiming to be a cook, he showed images of meatballs and asserted that vegan meatballs, e.g. those made with courgette and parsley, 'were not real meatballs' just like non-traditional family models, e.g. rainbow families, were not real families and so should not use the same term (ECR Seminar on Traditional Family 040220_FN).

In many cases, qualitative interviews and the ethnographic shadowing of participants exposed us to situations that were problematic, tense or unpleasant. This book is also a way of describing how we dealt with, processed and managed such situations.

Box 1.1 Quotations from the team research diary after coding radical-right MEP interviews and post-interview notes with right-wing actors

- 'First answer clearly sets the tone! It's very upsetting to read. 'me, myself and I'. I feel so sorry for X having to ask him equality questions!!!!! Well done for asking questions on gender equality!' (EUGenDem Research Diary 23 April 2020)
- 'Interesting stories about PG formation, fascinating how he keeps on saying Le Pen and AfD are not racist or antisemitic, how the people in Golden Dawn are nice'. (EUGenDem research diary, 10 Feb 2020)
- 'I felt the hierarchy, even though he was very polite. He bowed a bit as he shook my hand in the beginning and at the end. (…) I felt very awkward asking our 'gendered' questions—I physically felt irritation and displeasure 'radiating' off the participant when I asked about it, I also heard a small scoff from the

- assistant on the side'. (Post-interview note 5 Mar 2020)
- 'The MEP made a friendly impression on me although some of the things he talked about were really cringy for me (e.g. he is passionate about hunting). (…) I was surprised that he talked openly about the past of the Fratelli d'Italia as a direct descendant of the fascist party. But I guess, this is 'common knowledge' so no use denying it. (…) It's always disconcerting for me when right-wing people aren't nasty interpersonally to me as an interviewer (…). When a right-wing person is nice to me, I have cognitive dissonance'. (Post-interview note 12 May 2021)
- 'Interview was on skype. It was easier to set up than what I expected from the initial reaction to my first contact email. The participant replied that he can 'talk about foreign affairs, etc.(…) but that he doesn't understand the topics of gender' (Post-interview note 13 May 2021)
- 'I respected the MEP for having her own feminism, even if it was something that I fundamentally didn't agree with. I felt that it was a very legitimate complaint that she had felt looked down upon for being a stay-at-home mum'. (Post-interview note 11 Mar 2020)

By reflecting on a specific research process of data gathering and data analysis, we provide a complex picture of the role and methods of qualitative research in exploring informal institutions and studying the informality of political norms. Through qualitative research, we openly debate whether our findings call into question some of the traditional assumptions that underpin the 'mainstream' research. Our contribution lies in the inclusion of interviews and ethnographic data in our research process from a normatively feminist perspective. Therefore, we have added a distinctively 'gendered' look relative to the extant methodological literature, as well as anecdotes and diary entries that helped us reflect on the whole process.

QUALITATIVE AND FEMINIST RESEARCH IN PARLIAMENTS

Qualitative research is time and resource consuming. This is certainly reflected throughout the chapters in this book, where we illustrate how some of the burdens of such research can be eased by reviewing the necessary preparatory steps. These include, for example, gaining familiarity with the parliament and recruiting participants, and structuring the different stages of data analysis, such as coding or the interpretation of results. In key respects, the book takes a practical approach to the theoretical and methodological insights explored in the extant literature, which generally fall into three categories: (1) extensive handbooks on qualitative research, (2) wide-ranging handbook-style volumes on feminist research; (3) individual chapters in larger volumes or peer-reviewed journal publications dedicated only to aspects of parliamentary studies or gendered research.

Research publications and compilations on parliamentary studies, like Benoît and Rozenberg's (2020) *Handbook of Parliamentary Studies: Interdisciplinary Approaches to Legislatures* (Edward Elgar Publishing, 2020), Denzin and Lincoln's (2011) *Sage Handbook of qualitative research* or Leavy's (2020, Second Edition) *Oxford Handbook of Qualitative Research*, explore the research process by focusing on methodological considerations and their implications. The former provides an interdisciplinary output on parliamentarism from history, law and political economy to sociology and anthropology, whilst the latter two are mammoth volumes on state-of-the-art theory and operationalisation of qualitative inquiry from a methodological standpoint.

Notable volumes in the second category, to which our research owes intellectual gratitude, include Brooke Ackerly and Jacqui True's *Doing Feminist Research in Political and Social Science* (Red Globe Press, 2020) and Maureen McHugh's *Feminist Qualitative Research: Working toward Transforming Science and Social Justice* (2020). The former has a strong feminist theory and International Relations focus. It describes how a feminist research ethic can enrich the research process from start to finish, by simultaneously being a guide for feminist research ethics. The authors link the core elements of feminist research ethics with being attentive to the power of the social and political context, epistemology, boundaries and relationships, as well as situating the researcher with nonlinear research processes. Similarly, the latter offers an extensive overview of feminist research, naming validity and voice as particular challenges in the conduct of feminist qualitative research. She predicts the future of feminist research to be within multidisciplinary collaborations that contribute to the adoption of new perspectives and methods that ignore boundaries set by traditional disciplines that have served to restrict how research is conducted. Other works of significance include Tungohan and Catungal (2022) who address the most contemporary developments in virtual qualitative research in the context of the pandemic, and Bennett (2021), who echoes McHugh on the future of feminist qualitative research in considering what open science means for research methodologies that have historically been a home for transgressive and radical questioning.

Whilst building on this methodological richness, we nonetheless find a major lacuna: namely, the absence of a practical and accessible approach to the research process in the field and what follows it. Our volume is a succinct and hands-on monograph-guide to qualitative research in parliaments with an attendant reflexive attitude that transparently explores the successes and drawbacks of a research process in the European Parliament. As a team effort, the volume offers a coherent, yet multifaceted perspective on the research processes outlined in other publications. Furthermore, it has the advantage of accounting for major changes in research circumstances that arose due to the Covid-19 pandemic.

OUTLINE OF THE BOOK

This book has seven chapters and is structured around the two main vectors of qualitative research: data gathering and data analysis. We respond to the demand for greater critical methodological transparency by offering unique insights with detailed discussions of the strategies, decisions and tools we employed. Moreover, we reflect on the practicalities and technicalities applied in the collection, management, analysis and interpretation of a comprehensive dataset, consisting of various types of qualitative data: 140 interviews, ethnographic fieldnotes and document data gathered for the study of political groups over five years by six researchers. We explain the pros and cons of undertaking collaborative qualitative work by detailing the different stages of collective data gathering, team data coding and the interpretation of the results for individual and co-authored studies.

This chapter has introduced our focus and purpose, by explaining its hands-on approach to research and outlining its qualitative interpretive methodological nature. Chapter 2 on the *Set up of The European*

Parliament provides an overview of the existing research on the European Parliament and its political groups, as well as key information on the Parliament as a setting for qualitative research. It also provides key preliminary insights about conducting qualitative research in the European Parliament by engaging with key concepts and discussing them in the unique context of the European Parliament. In addition, we stress the high level of informality in the parliamentary work of the European Parliament, highlighting the contributions qualitative research makes to a field still largely dominated by quantitative research. The study of everyday dynamics and informal practices reinforces the importance of utilising a qualitative toolkit and data from interviews and ethnography, as well as broadening the range of research participants beyond political elites to include parliamentary staff.

Chapter 3 is the last of the background chapters. Here we introduce our research data and highlight the methodological innovations they generated to understand genderedness and intersecting (in)equalities in the European Parliament. The chapter outlines our two phases of data collection: a pilot study and the main data-gathering period. The variety of the data are emphasised by tables which illustrate the distribution by gender and nationality, as well as the political group affiliation and role of the research participants in the European Parliament. We explain and demonstrate the recording practices and techniques for parliamentary ethnography we employed, which elicited such a detailed understanding of informal political group dynamics. Finally, we consider how the research data was processed, archived and categorised, drawing on valuable lessons from the pilot study.

The main analytical chapters of the book—Chapters 4 to 7—provide details on the data gathering and analysis. Chapter 4 *How was data gathered? Doing research interviews and ethnography* describes the process of gathering data for research interviews and ethnography. First, we discuss the ethical review process and the impacts of the General Data Protection Regulation on interviews and ethnography. Chapter 4 also provides a detailed overview of the selection and recruitment of interviewees, how the interviews were conducted and describes the preparatory steps we took prior to the interviews. It also offers various ethnographic practices that researchers can use in parliamentary research, which is especially pertinent in light of Covid-19, and the impact this had on how the interviews were conducted and how the European Parliament operated in general.

In the first of two chapters that delve into the specificities of data analysis, Chapter 5 *Coding the data*, presents the strategies we used, and didn't use, to code dense interview, ethnographic and document data. Importantly, we generate important pointers regarding the use of software tools for qualitative analysis and highlight the intricacies of using such tools as a team with concrete examples. Additionally, we outline the technical and logistical issues that we faced when coding data collaboratively.

We move on to key methodological steps and strategies we employed for the interpretation of data. Chapter 6 *Interpreting the data*, provides a guide to conducting qualitative analysis driven by research questions that are intrinsically constructivist, interpretivist and/or post-structuralist. Here we are concerned with moving beyond coding and transforming our analysis into material that can be used to produce scientific studies for peer-reviewed publications. We cover the practical steps such as exporting code reports from ATLAS.ti and reviewing them in a collaborative fashion. It also includes a critical review of epistemological reflections that pertain to interpreting qualitative data. In this respect, the chapter not only excavates the specificities of how frames and discourses were interpreted from coded qualitative data but also how formal and informal practices were interpreted from 'texts'.

Our concluding chapter offers an open-ended discussion on future venues for qualitative research in political institutions in general and the European Parliament in particular. In summarising the key elements of the book, we stress the informality of many procedures, practices and mechanisms we witnessed and discuss their meaning for transparency and democracy. We also provide an open and thorough discussion of what we would do differently given the luxury of hindsight, offering our thoughts on the future direction for qualitative research in the European Parliament.

Reference

Ackerly, B. A., & True, J. (2020). *Doing feminist research in political and social science* (2nd edn.). Red Globe Press

Ahrens, P., Elomäki, A., & Kantola, J. (2022). *European parliament's political groups in turbulent times*. Palgrave MacMillan.

Bennett, E. A. (2021). Open science from a qualitative, feminist perspective: Epistemological dogmas and a call for critical examination. *Psychology of Women Quarterly, 45*(4), 448–456.

Benoît, C., & Rozenberg, O. (2020). *Handbook of parliamentary studies: Interdisciplinary approaches to legislatures.* Edward Elgar Publishing

Chappell, L., & Mackay, F. (2021). Feminist critical friends: Dilemmas of feminist engagement with governance and gender reform agendas. *European Journal of Politics and Gender, 4*(3), 321–340.

Chappell, L. (2020). Doing elite interviews in feminist research: Confessions of a born-again observationist. In P. Wadds, N. Apoifis, S. Schmeidl, & K. Spurway (Eds.), *Navigating fieldwork in the social sciences: Stories of danger, risk and reward* (pp. 129–145). Palgrave Macmillan.

Denzin, N. K., & Lincoln, Y. S. (2011). *The Sage handbook of qualitative research.* Sage.

Gaweda, B., Ahrens, P., Kantola, J., Berthet, V., & Miller, C. (2022, July 6–8). *Real science or witchcraft? Doing feminist research in the European parliament.* Paper presented at the European Conference on Politics & Gender (ECPG), Ljubljana

Kantola, J., Elomäki, A., Gaweda, B., Miller, C., Ahrens, P., & Berthet, V. (2023). "It's like shouting to a brick wall": Normative whiteness and racism in the European parliament. *American Political Science Review, 117*(1), 184–199.

Leavy, P. (2020). *The oxford handbook of qualitative research.* Oxford University Press.

McHugh, M. C. (2020). Feminist qualitative research: Working toward transforming science and social justice. In P. Leavy (Eds.), *The oxford handbook of qualitative research* (2nd edn.). New York: Oxford University Press.

Tungohan, E., & Catungal, J. P. (2022). Virtual qualitative research using transnational feminist queer methodology: The challenges and opportunities of zoom-based research during moments of crisis. *International Journal of Qualitative Methods, 21.* https://doi.org/10.1177/16094069221090062

CHAPTER 2

Set up: The European Parliament

Abstract Prior to conducting any research, it is crucial to understand and familiarise oneself with the research context and setting. The chapter provides an overview of the existing research on the European Parliament and its political groups, as well as key information on the Parliament as a setting for qualitative research. Following the step-by-step approach of the book, Chapter 2 provides the readers with key preliminary insights about the European Parliament with regard to conducting qualitative research. It engages with key concepts in qualitative research on parliaments and discusses them in light of the uniqueness of the European Parliament. Specifically, the cultural and linguistic diversity and its highly technical legislative process and complex institutional context make the European Parliament a rich albeit challenging site of qualitative research. The chapter stresses the high level of informality in the parliamentary work of the European Parliament and highlights the contributions qualitative research makes to a field still largely dominated by quantitative research. The study of everyday dynamics and informal practices reinforces the importance of utilising a qualitative toolkit and data, like interviews and ethnography, and that of broadening the range of research participants to parliamentary staff from political elites only.

Keywords European Parliament · Political groups · Informality · Institutional context · Research context

© The Author(s) 2023
V. Berthet et al., *Guide to Qualitative Research in Parliaments*,
https://doi.org/10.1007/978-3-031-39808-7_2

INTRODUCTION

The initial stage of most research is to gain familiarity with the context and the setting—acquainting yourself with previous research findings, establishing what is known about it thus far and discerning where the knowledge gaps might be. Covering these various aspects of the existing literature is a fundamental building block of research as it helps to: (a) defend and explain one's own research focus and topic; (b) pinpoint what is already known and what might be missing; (c) compare and contrast the empirical findings to the ones that have already been made elsewhere and (d) draw preliminary conclusions about theoretical, conceptual, methodological and empirical contributions. These steps are very much the backbone of any thesis or scientific article—nothing frustrates and disappoints reviewers more than an evidently untrue claim that a subject has not been researched before.

The questions we wanted answered in relation to this initial scene-setting phase, included how the European Parliament was working within a wider frame of reference, and what it meant for our qualitative research. For us, parliament was the larger field; within which the gendered practices, processes and outputs of political groups were situated. Our main research site was thus the European Parliament located in Brussels and Strasbourg and its informal adjacent spaces. As a research group, we spent the first years in a fortnightly reading group sharing and discussing the existing research on the parliament, and in particular the political groups. This chapter introduces the valuable insights that a first research step like this generates.

WHAT KIND OF PARLIAMENT?

There are many good books about the European Parliament (Corbett et al., 2016; Ripoll Servent, 2018), specialised journal articles and even publications about specific aspects of the European Parliament (Whitaker, 2011; Yordanova, 2013). Of greater significance to us, was an edited volume on gendering the European Parliament that we had contributed to, as well as journal articles and book chapters about the gendered character of how the parliament functions (Ahrens & Rolandsen Agustín, 2019). Our specific angle was to focus on the political groups of the parliament from a gender perspective. Understanding our research setting, meant familiarising ourselves with the actors and structural cleavages within and between the political groups in the parliament. Interestingly, prior to our edited volume, there were no books that covered the full spectrum of these political groups (Ahrens, Elomäki & Kantola, 2022), and certainly no books on political groups and gender. There were, however, a lot more articles and book chapters on political groups than we had anticipated.

One pertinent characterisation when undertaking qualitative research on parliaments is to distinguish between a *debating parliament* and a *working parliament* (Lord, 2018; Tiilikainen & Wiesner, 2016). In contrast to the UK House of Commons which is commonly depicted as a classic chamber focused on debating (see, e.g. Miller, 2021, 2022a, b), the European Parliament is most often characterised as a committee-focused working parliament. Undoubtedly, these are very specific examples and all parliaments have characteristics of both types, arguably both are vital for a functioning parliamentary democracy, yet such distinctions can serve as pointers to why certain factors might be seen as particularly important to research participants. Whilst committees form the basis of policy work in a working parliament, understanding how power works demands being attentive to policy leadership positions such as rapporteurs, coordinators and committee chairs. The notion of a working parliament implicitly suggests that parliamentary majorities and coalitions are policy specific and flexible, as opposed to being fixed and centralised in debating parliaments (Miller, 2022a, b). Consensus and coalition building, trust and networking have been shown to be important in the European Parliament in a number of studies. Despite this, the influx of radical-right populists, Eurosceptics and anti-gender politicians brings in actors who disrupt the logics that prioritised the plenary as a main site of their action, and who are dismissive, or closed off from, traditional political dynamics (see, e.g. Brack, 2018; Kantola & Miller, 2021; Kantola & Lombardo, 2021).

There has been a long-standing debate about the uniqueness of the European Parliament relative to national parliaments (Hix et al., 2007). After the significant increase and solidification of its legislative and budgetary powers, as well as its important scrutiny functions, the debate has to some extent been settled. Suffice it to say, the European Parliament is surely as powerful, if not more powerful, than national parliaments, even if it still lacks the right to initiate legislation. This does not, however, mean that unique features are somewhat lacking. On the contrary, its distinctive characteristics make both working in, and researching, the parliament interesting and more challenging than doing similar research at the national level.

With 705 Members of the European Parliament (MEPs), the parliament is relatively big (for comparisons to other parliaments see De Feo & Jacobs, 2021). More significantly, MEPs come from 27 member states, variant political parties and speak 24 official languages. The parliament's multilingual character, and the translation practices that have developed around it, is indeed one of its most unique characteristics (Bartlomiejczyk, 2020; Ringe, 2022). The parliament is also multicultural and constitutes an amalgamation of 27 national political traditions and as many gender regimes. In this respect, some political groups such as the European People's Party (EPP), possess 176 MEPs, which makes them larger than some national parliaments. Yet, the parliament is very homogenous when it comes to differences other than the gender with only 3 per cent of MEPs representing people of colour (Kantola et al., 2023).

The European Parliament is also unique because of the highly technical nature of the legislation that it deals with, and the complexity of the institutional context—the interinstitutional relations to the Council and the Commission—in which it is embedded (Christiansen et al., 2021: 484). The challenges for MEPs' work are well known: the European Parliament is a co-legislator together with the Council, and it engages primarily with Commission's proposals, yet MEPs have far fewer staff at its disposal, and is heavily reliant on external experts and lobbyists. Whilst MEPs can delve deeper into matters that they are either responsible for as rapporteurs, shadows, committees chairs or members, they simply cannot familiarise themselves with all the technical details relating to every vote and report. Instead, they are given voting lists and tend to follow these on most matters. Taken together, this places unique challenges of complexity for both working and researching in the parliament.

The European Parliament is governed by Rules of Procedure that have been frequently amended. As a research project, we spent extended periods reading these rules and discussing them along with some excellent articles tracing the significance of rule changes in the parliament (Brack & Costa, 2018a, b; Kreppel, 2002). It was soon apparent that the European Parliament is extensively self-regulated. It was interesting to discover that the Parliament completely determined its procedures by being in charge of its own rules, and the regularity with which they had been changed. Moreover, how these changes reflected shifts in the power of the parliament—with the direction of travel revealing a trajectory which bestowed greater power to political groups, at the expense of individual MEPs (Brack & Costa, 2018a). Within this shift of power, we also found out that many issues were not governed by the rules, or if they were it was ambiguous, leaving their interpretation open to the political groups or informal rules and agreements.

The high level of informality in terms of informal practices and institutional processes suggests that qualitative research, using interviews and ethnography, is likely to be better suited to revealing what is going on beyond the formal rules (see Box 2.1 and Box. 2.2 below). Other scholars, in what constituted a turn to informal politics and micropolitics, used these methods and approaches to bring new insights to a field traditionally dominated by quantitative studies of voting patterns and formal rules (Brack, 2018; Busby, 2013; Landorff, 2019; Ripoll Servent, 2018; Ripoll Servant & Panning, 2019; Wiesner, 2018, 2019). To tap into this, we draw heavily on Feminist Institutionalism as a theoretical and methodological approach to define 'formal' and 'informal' institutions, the relations between them and their significance for societal change (Waylen, 2017; Chappell and Mackay, 2017). Feminist institutionalism does not rest content with simply the analytical relationships between formality and informality but enables making deeper excursions into rules. Used in this way, it has been able to get a more nuanced reading of the 'everyday' dynamics of parliaments (Miller, 2021).

Box 2.1 Political Groups Formation

Whilst the powers of the European Parliament increased, little research was devoted to the formation of the political groups within it. With the political struggles of recent years and the rise of radical-right populism, a proper re-evaluation of the functioning and importance of political groups within the European Parliament was necessary. Drawing on 130 research interviews conducted with MEPs, political groups and parliamentary staff in 2018–2019 in the 8th and 9th parliaments, Ahrens and Kantola (2022) analysed precisely political group formation processes in the European Parliament. The findings stress the lack of formal rules in this prominent political performance and highlight the need to study informal practices. They found informal practices to be widespread in how groups come together. Group formation is shaped by the objective of maximising their size, sometimes at the expense of group unity. In turn, the negotiation of leadership positions varies across groups, with some using more standardised practices whilst others took decisions on a quasi-ad-hoc basis. Further, left-leaning groups tended to prioritise the objective of securing unified policy positions when forming their collective identity, whilst others emphasised the importance of common values at the expense of unified policy positions. On the other hand, radical-right populist groups placed greater emphasis on accommodating divergent national viewpoints and expressed a preference for open voting, without any motivation to increase policy coherence. The discussion underscores the need to understand political group formation not solely within the framework of the European Parliament but also in light of political dynamics at the group level—which dynamics are made visible by qualitative tools and methods.

For more, see Ahrens and Kantola (2022).

Box 2.2 Policy-Making Processes

Within the European Parliament's legislative process, political groups hold a crucial function. Scholars have given several accounts for the high degree of voting cohesion within groups, whilst few have explored the mechanism through which the groups arrive at their policy positions initially. Due to the internal heterogeneity of the groups, the negotiation of policy preferences within the groups become 'all the more relevant for supranational democracy' (Elomäki et al., 2022: 74). In the chapter 'Democratic Practices and Political Dynamics of Intra-Group Policy Formation in the European Parliament', Elomäki et al. (2022) ask how the groups formulate group lines and policy positions and what impact this dynamic has on democratic decision-making and intra-group democracy in the European Parliament. The findings indicate that political groups with greater ability to influence the position of the Parliament tend to formulate policy in a more centralised and hierarchical manner. For instance, the largest groups—namely the centre-left Group of the Progressive Alliance of Socialists and Democrats (S&D) and centre-right Group of the European People's Party (EPP)—placed great emphasis on having a unified group stance, with formal regulations requiring MEPs to support the group line. For the centre-right liberal Renew Europe and the Greens/European Free Alliance (Greens/EFA), a unified group line was essential, but unlike the two largest groups, not enforced through formal regulations. Groups on the left such as the Left Group (GUE/NGL) lacked formal rules and interviewees highlighted big differences between national party delegations due to the confederal nature of the group. Regarding eurosceptic parties, their formal regulations underlined that MEPs may vote 'as they see fit'. Amongst the formal and informal processes that influence democratic practices, Elomäki et al. (2022) point out how the formal rule of gender balance in groups is limited by informal rules of seniority, resulting in men being overrepresented. Moreover, the research points at an important dynamic; the role of political groups in policy-making is increasing, whilst the power of committee experts is decreasing. Notably, a handful of MEPs such as group leaders take key decisions in the group and leaders of large national party delegations are decisive actors. Elomäki et al. (2022) conclude that in the European Parliament, the pursuit of influence through a unified position can sometimes contradict the principles of inclusion, participation and deliberation, even in smaller groups. Such contradictions emerged from qualitative methodologies.

In addition to being a working parliament, the European Parliament could also be termed an 'equality parliament'—understanding the structures, processes and actors behind this has been central to our endeavour. Here, our challenge differed from getting a sense of the parliament as a working parliament. Some of our own previous research contributed to knowledge about the European Parliament as an equality parliament (see Kantola, 2010; Kantola & Rolandsen Agustín, 2016, 2019; Ahrens, 2016; Ahrens & Rolandsen Agustín, 2021; Warasin et al., 2019; Ahrens, Meier & Rolandsen Agustín, 2022), and as a consequence, this project has involved digging deeper and going beyond what we thought we already knew. The notion of the European Parliament as an equality parliament is built around several dimensions and includes, for example, the high numbers of women MEPs when compared to national parliaments (Aldrich & Daniel, 2020; Fortin-Rittberger & Rittberger, 2014; Lühiste & Kenny, 2016); well established feminist governance structures of the parliament including a Committee for Women's Rights and Gender Equality, an internationally rare strong commitment to gender mainstreaming (Ahrens, 2016, 2019; Elomäki & Kantola, 2022; Kantola & Lombardo, 2023; Elomäki & Ahrens, 2022); successes in defending gender policy, strengthening its provisions vis-a-vis the Council and the Commission; speaking out, not just for gender equality, but also for LGBTQI rights and anti-racism (Mos, 2018; Ahrens, Gaweda, & Kantola, 2022; Kantola et al., 2023).

Despite the increasing interest in, and number of scholarly articles about, political groups in the broader milieux of the European Parliament, we were quickly able to identify notable gaps. Some of these could be explained by the fact that political groups were considered as actors within the formal landscapes of working and equality parliaments, rather than as scenes or stages for policy-making and politics, including feminist politics, and as more coherent wholes whilst voting and submitting amendments. Academic research had been able to tell whether they were cohesive, and how well they built coalitions, but what we were interested in was the 'intra-group' dynamics of the political groups. What kind of stages did they occupy for the daily work of their MEPs and staff? What norms and structures governed them when they were formed, when they formulated policy and took decisions? What were the political cultures of each group? What was the significance of national delegations and political parties, did some delegations dominate over others? Moreover, how were all of these norms and structures gendered, and how did that impact the effectiveness of political work? Eventually, answers to such questions helped us to disaggregate the parliament's equality reputation to reveal the reality of gendered inequalities, the diverging ways of advancing gender perspectives and policy at the political group level (see, e.g. Ahrens, Gaweda, & Kantola, 2022; Elomäki, 2021; Kantola, 2022) and the parliament's reputation as a working parliament on the basis that political groups had widely different practices in policy-making (Elomäki et al., 2022; Elomäki & Gaweda, 2022) (see Box 2.3 below).

Box 2.3 Gendered Leadership

The issue of gender equality as both a norm and a policy question is a highly politicised and contested topic in the European Parliament. The political groups of the European Parliament are sharply divided in their support and promotion of gender equality, with one-quarter represented by radical-right populists who firmly oppose gender equality norms and express their dissent both directly and indirectly in plenary debates. In the chapter 'Gender-related leadership in the political groups of the European Parliament', Kantola and Miller (2022) contribute to the discussion on gender in the European Parliament by focusing on how leadership positions provided by political groups fail to provide equal opportunities for MEPs. The study draws on a large sample of interviews (n = 123) with MEPs and staff, covering political, policy and administrative leadership within political groups during the 8th (2014–2019) and 9th (2019–2024) legislatures. The research shows that despite the European Parliament's reputation for gender equality, men still dominate political leadership. The leadership of national party delegations (NDPs) contains hidden gendered structures, with significantly fewer women in leadership positions. In addition, although policy leadership (i.e. committee chairs and coordinators) is relatively gender-balanced, the Group of the European People's Party (EPP) is an exception in this matter. Despite progress, gendered norms and practices still limit the scope of action within leadership positions, highlighting the challenges of achieving gender equality in the European Parliament. Kantola and Miller (2022) reveal that women are underrepresented in administrative leadership roles, i.e. as Secretary Generals of political groups. Whilst administrative leadership positions are clear on paper, with nominally democratic voting within political groups, gender concerns are routinely overshadowed by power politics, trust networks and the prioritisation of seniority. The pivotal function of Secretary Generals has received limited scholarly attention. Thus, securing interviews with these key personnel allowed valuable insights on their role.

For more, see Kantola and Miller (2022).

One aspect of our research was to gather data, not only from MEPs but also from parliamentary staff. Christiansen et al. (2021) noted how under-researched the administrative dimensions of representative institutions have hitherto been. For them, this was problematic because the 'influence and effectiveness of democratic politics depends not only on the activity of elected members, but also on the kind of the administrative support upon which mandates can be reliably carried out' (Christiansen et al., 2021: 478). In the European Parliament, administrative support staff consists of various types. First, civil servants who work at the parliamentary level for committees, the secretariat, or the political groups, and second, there are the personal assistants (APAs, accredited personal assistants) of the MEPs. The latter are governed by different work contracts, norms and power relations. APAs, for example, are highly reliant on the MEPs who recruited them and are expected to be loyal to them (Pegan, 2017). The other administrative staff are expected to display political neutrality and institutional loyalty, despite often working in and for political groups. The high level of turn-over in European Parliament elections, close to 50 per cent, means that the parliamentary administration provides 'continuity and institutional memory for the legislature' (Christiansen et al., 2021: 478). We also found this to be the case with the Secretaries of General (SG) of the political groups, who played a pivotal role in the weeks following an election when political groups were formed and new MEPs took up their jobs (Ahrens & Kantola, 2022; Kantola & Miller, 2022).

Understanding the role of administrative staff is equally crucial for gender research. It fits well with the recent turn in gender and politics scholarship where parliaments have been understood as gendered workplaces (see Erikson & Verge, 2022). This scholarship has underpinned the idea that treating parliaments as special representative institutions outside the social norms and laws that govern normal working life, can be harmful for gender equality. By doing so, members of administrative staff, who are sometimes even more vulnerable than politicians, can be exposed to unchecked and unmonitored sexual harassment (see Miller, 2021; Berthet, 2022; Berthet & Kantola, 2021). Sexual harassment has been comprehensively documented as a deeply rooted problem in European parliaments, such as Westminster (Collier & Raney, 2018; Krook, 2018; Miller, 2021) and the European Parliament. Significantly, the position and counter-action by parliamentary staff in the European Parliament was absolutely crucial in tackling the issue (Berthet, 2022; Berthet &

Kantola, 2021). Indeed, it has been the personal assistants of MEPs, the APAs, who have played a key role in these struggles (Berthet, 2022). On a more general methodological level, interviewing those who seem to have less, little or no power can often reveal more about the exercise of power than those who have it.

A number of academic books and articles have been written about MEPs based on qualitative in-depth interviews with MEPs. This has a number of positives: it is clearly possible to undertake elite interviews with MEPs (e.g. Brack, 2018; Cullen, 2018; Kantola & Rolandsen Agustín, 2019; Sarikakis, 2003; Landorff, 2019; Daniel, 2015; Whitaker, 2011; Wodak et al., 2009) as well as participant observation and/or parliamentary ethnography in Brussels and Strasbourg (Abélès, 1992; Busby, 2013, 2014), of EU institutions more generally (Firat, 2019; Lewicki, 2016; Mérand, 2021; Shore, 2000) and MEPs in their constituency (Poyet, 2018). Slightly more negatively, the European Parliament's unique nature has been a challenging environment for qualitative interviews. Marc Abélès (1992) noted the difficulties of doing parliamentary work in the European Parliament, whilst some previous studies have only been based on relatively small numbers of MEP interviews. For example, Pauline Cullen (2018) interviewed six Irish female MEPs, Kantola and Rolandsen Agustín (2019) interviewed 18 female Danish and Finnish MEPs. In contrast, Landorff interviewed a healthy 42 MEPs (and 8 staff members) whilst Brack (2018) had a much larger sample of 101 Eurosceptics MEPs and 32 other MEPs and staff.

There are key challenges to carrying out qualitative interviews or parliamentary ethnography in the European Parliament. First, the parliament sits in many locations, most notably Brussels and Strasbourg, but also online during the Covid-19 pandemic; in the case of physical locations, researchers must be able to move between different places (De Feo & Jacobs, 2021). Second, the parliament is multilingual and one cannot assume interviews can be conducted in English, nor can translations be taken at face value; they can be political and meaning can easily be lost in the process (Bartlomiejczyk, 2020; Ringe, 2022). The multilingual character of the parliament can be even more challenging for parliamentary ethnographies and methods such as shadowing, where a MEP being shadowed can use languages not understood by the researcher (Miller, 2022a, b). Third, the parliament buildings are governed by a security system and can be entered only through security and accreditation, namely an invitation or study permit. More documentation, notably criminal records, is sought from researchers outside the Schengen area. Fourth! most MEPs are extremely busy, and time-pressured with their work, which makes eliciting interviews difficult (Busby, 2013; Sarikakis, 2003).

CONCLUSION

This chapter described the first stages of the research we undertook on the European Parliament's political groups. It consisted of understanding the research setting and context, which for us was getting to know the European Parliament, its political groups, actors and the cities of Brussels and Strasbourg. We have emphasised the importance of getting to know the intricacies of the research setting and how the existing literature had conceptualised and understood it. For us, it mattered that we fully grasped the powers and competences of the parliament, but more importantly, it mattered to understand the political cleavages and power dynamics of and between parliamentary actors. As a result, we saw the necessity to extend our focus beyond elected MEPs, to parliamentary staff and members of the administration, whose influence or expertise is less known, but whose knowledge of the parliament, practices and policies were critical to achieve a more nuanced account.

REFERENCE

Abélès, M. (1992). *La vie quotidienne au Parlement Européen*. Hachette.

Ahrens, P. (2016). The Committee on women's rights and gender equality in the European parliament: Taking advantage of institutional power play. *Parliamentary Affairs, 69*(4), 778–793.

Ahrens, P., & Rolandsen Agustín, L. (2019). *Gendering the European parliament: Introducing structures, policies, and practices*. Rowman & Littlefield.

Ahrens, P., & Kantola, J. (2022). Political group formation in the European parliament: Negotiating democracy and gender. *Party Politics Advance Online Publication*. https://doi.org/10.1177/13540688221106295

Ahrens, P., Elomäki, A., & Kantola, J. (2022). *European parliament's political groups in turbulent times*. Palgrave Macmillan.

Ahrens, P., Gaweda, B., & Kantola, J. (2022). Reframing the language of human rights? Political group contestations on women's and LGBTQI rights in European parliament debates. *Journal of European Integration, 44*(6), 803–819.

Ahrens, P., Meier, P., & Rolandsen Agustín, L. (2022). The European parliament and gender equality: An analysis of achievements based on the concept of power. *Journal of Common Market Studies, Advance Online Publication.* https://doi.org/10.1111/jcms.13446

Ahrens, P., & Rolandsen Agustín, L. (2021). European parliament. In G. Abels, A. Krizsán, H. MacRae, & A. van der Vleuten (Eds.), *The Routledge handbook of gender and EU politics* (pp. 107–119). Routledge.

Aldrich, A. S., & Daniel, W. T. (2020). The consequences of quotas: Assessing the effect of varied gender quotas on legislator experience in the European parliament. *Politics & Gender, 16*(3), 738–767.

Bartłomiejczyk, M. (2020). How much noise can you make through an interpreter? A case study on racist discourse in the European parliament. *Interpreting, 22*(2), 238–261.

Berthet, V. (2022). Mobilization against sexual harassment in the European parliament: The MeTooEP campaign. *European Journal of Women's Studies, 29*(2), 331–346.

Berthet, V., & Kantola, J. (2021). Gender, violence and political institutions: Struggles over sexual harassment in the European Parliament. *Social Politics, 28*(1), 143–167.

Brack, N. (2018). Euroscepticism in the European parliament. In N. Brack (Ed.), *Opposing Europe in the European parliament: Rebels and radicals in the chamber* (pp. 51–81). Palgrave Macmillan.

Brack, N., & Costa, O. (2018a). The EP through the lens of legislative studies: Recent debates and new perspectives. *Journal of Legislative Studies, 24*(1), 1–178.

Brack, N., & Costa, O. (2018b). Democracy in parliament vs. democracy through parliament? Defining the rules of the game in the European parliament. *The Journal of Legislative Studies, 24*(1), 51–71

Busby, A. (2013). "Normal parliament": Exploring the organisation of everyday political life in an MEP's office. *Journal of Contemporary European Research, 9*(1), 94–115.

Busby, A. (2014). "Bursting the Brussels bubble": Using ethnography to explore the European parliament as a transnational political field. *Perspectives on European Politics and Society, 14*(2), 203–222.

Chappell, L., & Mackay, F. (2017). What's in a name? Mapping the terrain of informal institutions and gender politics. In G. Waylen (Ed.), *Gender and informal institutions* (pp. 23–44). Rowman & Littlefield.

Christiansen, T., Griglio, E., & Lupo, N. (2021). Making representative democracy work: The role of parliamentary administrations in the European Union. *The Journal of Legislative Studies, 27*(4), 477–493.

Collier, C. N., & Raney, T. (2018). Understanding sexism and sexual harassment in politics: A comparison of Westminster parliaments in Australia, the United Kingdom, and Canada. *Social Politics, 25*(3), 432–455.

Corbett, R., Jacobs, F. & Neville, D. (2016). *The European parliament* (9th edn.). John Harper

Cullen, P. (2018). Irish female members of the European parliament: Critical actors for women's interests? *Politics & Gender, 14*(3), 483–511.

Daniel, W. T. (2015). *Career behaviour and the European parliament: All roads lead through Brussels?* Oxford University Press.

De Feo, A., & Jacobs, F. (2021). The European experience of parliamentary administrations in comparative perspective. *The Journal of Legislative Studies, 27*(4), 554–576.

Elomäki, A. (2021). "It's a total no-no": The strategic silence about gender in the European parliament's economic governance policies. *International Political Science Review, Advance Online Publication.* https://doi.org/10.1177/0192512120978329

Elomäki, A., Gaweda, B., & Berthet, V. (2022). Democratic practices and political dynamics of intra-group policy formation in the European parliament. In P. Ahrens, A. Elomäki, & J. Kantola (Eds.), *European parliament's political groups in turbulent times* (pp. 73–96). Palgrave Macmillan.

Elomäki, A., & Ahrens, P. (2022). Contested gender mainstreaming in the European parliament: Political groups and committees as gatekeepers. *European Journal of Politics and Gender, 5*(3), 322–340.

Elomäki, A., & Kantola, J. (2022). Feminist governance in the European parliament: The political struggle over the inclusion of gender in the EU's COVID-19 response. *Politics & Gender, 19*(2), 1–22.

Erikson, J., & Verge, T. (2022). Gender, power and privilege in the parliamentary workplace. *Parliamentary Affairs, 75*(1), 1–19.

Firat, B. (2019). *Diplomacy and lobbying during Turkey's Europeanisation: The private life of politics.* Manchester University Press

Fortin-Rittberger, J., & Rittberger, B. (2014). Do electoral rules matter? Explaining national differences in women's representation in the European Parliament. *European Union Politics, 15*(4), 496–520.

Hix, S., Noury, A. G., & Roland, G. (2007). *Democratic politics in the European parliament.* Cambridge University Press.

Kantola, J. (2010). *Gender and the European Union.* Bloomsbury Publishing.

Kantola, J. (2022). Parliamentary politics and polarisation around gender: Tackling inequalities in political groups in the European parliament. In P. Ahrens, A. Elomäki, & J. Kantola (Eds.), *European parliament's political groups in turbulent times* (pp. 221–243). Palgrave Macmillan.

Kantola, J., Elomäki, A., Gaweda, B., Miller, C., Ahrens, P., & Berthet, V. (2023). "It's like shouting to a brick wall": Normative whiteness and racism in the European parliament. *American Political Science Review, 117*(1), 184–199.

Kantola, J., & Lombardo, E. (2021). Opposition strategies of right populists against gender equality in a polarized European parliament. *International Political Science Review, 42*(5), 565–579.

Kantola, J., & Lombardo, E. (2023). The European parliament as a gender equality actor: A contradictory forerunner. In M. Sawer, L. Banaszak, J. True, & J. Kantola (Eds.), *Handbook of feminist governance* (pp. 299–310). Edward Elgar Publishing.

Kantola, J., & Miller, C. (2021). Party politics and radical right populism in the European parliament: Analysing political groups as democratic actors. *Journal of Common Market Studies, 59*(4), 782–801.

Kantola, J., & Miller, C. (2022). Gendered leadership in the European parliament's political groups. In H. Müller & I. Tömmel (Eds.), *Women and leadership in the European Union* (pp. 150–169). Oxford University Press.

Kantola, J., & Rolandsen Agustín, L. (2016). Gendering transnational party politics: The case of European Union. *Party Politics, 22*(5), 641–651.

Kantola, J., & Rolandsen Agustín, L. (2019). Gendering the representative work of the European parliament: A political analysis of women MEP's perceptions of gender equality in party groups. *Journal of Common Market Studies, 57*(4), 768–786.

Kreppel, A. (2002). *The European parliament and supranational party system: A study in institutional development.* Cambridge University Press.

Krook, M. L. (2018). Westminster too: On sexual harassment in British politics. *The Political Quarterly, 89*(1), 65–72.

Landorff, L. (2019). *Inside European parliament politics: Informality, information and intergroups.* Palgrave Macmillan.

Lewicki, P. (2016). European bodies?: Class and gender dynamics among EU civil servants in Brussels. *Anthropological Journal of European Cultures, 25*(2), 116–138.

Lord, C. (2018). The European Parliament: A working parliament without a public? *The Journal of Legislative Studies, 24*(1), 34–50.

Lühiste, M., & Kenny, M. (2016). Pathways to power: Women's representation in the 2014 European parliament elections. *European Journal of Political Research, 55*(3), 626–641.

Mérand, F. (2021). *The political commissioner: A European ethnography.* Oxford University Press.

Miller, C. M. (2021). Parliamentary ethnography and feminist institutionalism: Gendering institutions–but how? *European Journal of Politics and Gender, 4*(3), 361–380.

Miller, C. (2022a). 'Ethno, Ethno, What?': Using ethnography to explore the European parliament's political groups in turbulent times. In P. Ahrens, A. Elomäki, & J. Kantola (Eds.), *European parliament's political groups in turbulent times* (pp. 245–266). Palgrave Macmillan.

Miller, C. M. (2022b). Between Westminster and Brussels: Putting the "parliament" in parliamentary ethnography. *Politics & Gender*, 1–27

Mos, M. (2018). The fight of the religious right in Europe: Old whines in new bottles European. *Journal of Politics and Gender*, *1*(3), 325–343.

Pegan, A. (2017). The role of personal parliamentary assistants in the European parliament. *West European Politics*, *40*(2), 295–315.

Poyet, C. (2018). Working at home: French MEPs' day-to-day practice of political representation in their district. *The Journal of Legislative Studies*, *24*(1), 109–126.

Ringe, N. (2022). *The language (s) of politics: Multilingual Multilingual policymaking in the European Union*. University of Michigan Press.

Ripoll Servent, A. (2018). *The European parliament*. Palgrave Macmillan.

Sarikakis, K. (2003). Feminist in Brussels A feminist in Brussels (and Glasgow, Berlin, Düsseldorf...). *European Journal of Women's Studies*, *10*(4), 423–441

Shore, C. (2000). *Building Europe: The cultural politics of European integration*. Routledge

Tiilikainen, T., & Wiesner, C. (2016). Towards a political theory of EU Parliamentarism. In P. Ihalainen, C. Ilie, & K. Palonen (Eds.), *Parliaments and parliamentarism. A comparative history of disputes on a European concept* (pp. 292–310). Berghahn Books

Ripoll Servent, A., & Panning, L. (2019). Eurosceptics in trilogue settings: Interest formation and contestation in the European Parliament. *West European Politics*, *42*(4), 755–775.

Warasin, M., Kantola, J., Agustín, L. S. R., & Coughlan, C. (2019). Politicisation of gender equality in the European parliament: Cohesion and inter-group coalitions in plenary and committees. In P. Ahrens & L. Rolandsen Agustín (Eds.), *Gendering the European parliament: Structures, policies, and practices* (pp. 141–158). Rowman & Littlefield International

Waylen, G. (2017). *Gender and informal institutions*. Rowman & Littlefield.

Whitaker, R. (2011). *The European Parliament's committees: National party influence and legislative empowerment*. Routledge

Wiesner, C. (2019). *Inventing the EU as a democratic polity*. Palgrave Macmillan.

Wiesner, C. (2018). The Micro-Politics of parliamentary powers: European parliament strategies for expanding its influence in the EU institutional system. *Journal of European Integration*, *40*(4), 375–391.

Wodak, R., de Cillia, R., Reisigl, M., & Liebhart, K. (2009). *Discursive construction of national identity*. Edinburgh University Press

Yordanova, N. (2013). *Organising the European parliament: The role of committees and their legislative influence*. ECPR Press

CHAPTER 3

Introducing Our Data

Abstract The data was gathered with the aim to generate empirical knowledge about gendered European party politics and the ways in which these affect the prospects for democracy and gender equality in Europe. It also aimed to innovate the study of formal and informal institutions and discourses in party politics. This chapter presents the data and highlights the methodological innovations they generated in the understanding of genderedness of the European Parliament. The chapter outlines how data collection occurred in two phases: a pilot study and the main data-gathering period. Overall, 140 interviews, 193 pages of fieldnotes and a wealth of internal documents from the European Parliament and its political groups were gathered during these two phases. Tables illustrate the distribution by gender and nationality, as well as the political group affiliation and role of the research participants in the European Parliament to stress the variety of the data. The chapter explains and demonstrates recording practices and techniques for parliamentary ethnography, which enabled a detailed understanding of informal political group dynamics. Finally, the chapter describes how the research data was processed, archived and categorised, drawing on lessons from the pilot study.

Keywords Empirical knowledge · Pilot study · Main data collection · Qualitative assessment · Methodological innovation

© The Author(s) 2023
V. Berthet et al., *Guide to Qualitative Research in Parliaments*,
https://doi.org/10.1007/978-3-031-39808-7_3

31

Introduction

Prior to a critical analysis of our findings, this chapter presents the data on which the remainder of this volume is based. We first outline the two phases of data collection, followed by a comprehensive overview of the data we gathered in its entirety. The final section is attentive to the logistics and technicalities of storing and archiving our data as well as lessons learned in these processes.

Research outcomes are dependent upon the way research questions are framed, the consideration of pre-existing textual data sources, time and practical skills (cf. Leavy, 2020), as well as more pragmatic issues such as access to participants. From the outset, our project was designed with two main stages of research in mind: (i) generating new empirical knowledge about the gendered character of European party politics and its impact on gender equality and democracy in Europe and (ii) methodological innovation in the study of formal and informal institutions and discourses in party politics.

Data collection commenced immediately when the project began. It consisted of two extensive qualitative fieldwork phases (see the following section for details): the pilot study (2018–2019) and the main data collection (2019–2022). The processes of data gathering and analysis were inextricably linked and developed over time from the pilot study to the main data collection, with the active participation and input by all team members. The project introduced, and implemented, methodological innovations that allowed us to gain a thorough empirical understanding of the various ways that gender manifests itself in the EP political groups. This was enabled by our data collection, the creation of a unique dataset and the systematic development of analytical schemes for filing and coding in an iterative team process, which we discuss in greater detail in the following chapters.

Two Phases of Data Collection: The Pilot and the Main Study

The initial data collection involved an extensive qualitative pilot study with expert and elite interviews from October 2018 to May 2019. This corresponded to the 8th parliamentary term in the EP (2014–2019). In total, we interviewed 54 MEPs and staff in the EP, covering all eight political groups of that parliamentary term and reflected gender parity amongst the interviewees. All our interviews were recorded with the permission of the interviewees. If the request to record was declined by the interviewee, then the interviewer took notes. The interview data was fully confidential, and interviewees were guaranteed full anonymity. Ethnographic fieldwork in the pilot study period allowed the team to gain a thicker volume of data, but with a finer-grained understanding of (in)formal political grouping dynamics. Overall, there were 104 pages of fieldnotes and 79 formal hours of shadowing and observations. In 2019, the team began the in-depth analysis of the interview data by developing codes for the different research questions (a more detailed discussion can be found in Chapters 4–6).

Following the pilot study, we held team meetings to reflect on our data sample. Overall, good lessons were learnt with a pilot study. We formulated the pilot period to avoid putting pressure on getting a high total sample, but rather to elicit necessary information about the process of data gathering in the EP. The pilot study provided useful material for analysis, and throughout the process, we learned, for instance, about the importance of the administrative leadership role played by the Secretary Generals in the political groups. It also gave room for reflection on the research field, allowing us to 'learn the ropes' of EP functioning. In this respect, we came to appreciate the value of responding to interviewees, asking follow-up questions and requesting follow-up meetings. We also identified 'black boxes' that stood out in the extant scholarship, for example, the workings of the Bureau and the Conference of Presidents. In light of the pilot study, we identified some new targets to pursue, such as shadow rapporteur meetings that take place during committee meetings, or the possibility of contacting group coordinators if we needed to request access. We also realised the value of being able to talk to the secretariat staff of committees who had a lot to say about political groups.

The pilot study allowed us to better define whom we wanted to target, and how we prioritised and scheduled our work. We then reached a general agreement about how to manage what would be a hectic schedule to complete the data gathering as soon as possible, given the time and geography constraints both for us and for our interviewees. On reflection, these pressures resulted in data that was less systematic than we had planned for. In addition, we had to resign ourselves to the fact that at times the interviews were more ad-hoc than we would have liked. Nevertheless, all the interviewees appreciated our flexibility in adjusting schedules to fit the interviewees' changing schedules and we always tried to ensure that another team member was available to 'take over' if necessary.

The pilot study was also invaluable to the important process of reviewing our interview questionnaires. Initially, the length of the interview guide proved an issue. On occasion, the interviewees' time constraints made it difficult to stick to, requiring us to be reflexive in the prioritisation of tasks and to improvise when necessary. However, at times it proved difficult to adjust the schedule when interruptions occurred during the interview. Thus, the main takeaway was to make sure we inserted enough flexibility into the schedule for the future—including multiple follow-up questions and variants depending on the interviewee, and questions that could be 'skipped' if necessary. The result was that we divided the interview schedule into 'core' questions and sub-questions that we could potentially miss.

In developing the process for the main data collection, we established the number of interviews we wanted to conduct. In team meetings, we decided to aim for ten interviews from each of the seven political groups in the 9th EP term, making 70 interviews altogether, each to include six MEPs, two accredited assistants and two political group staff members—whilst at the same time ensuring a gender balance. The main data collection was conducted between December 2019 and March 2020 (in person). Data gathering continued after the onset of the Covid-19 restrictions through online and telephone interviews between March 2020 and March 2022. In response to the changing circumstances, the team jointly developed questionnaires for MEPs and political group staff and also updated the interview schedules to include questions on current developments (e.g. ongoing Covid-19 restrictions and their implications for parliamentary work). In total, we interviewed 79 MEPs and staff in the main data collection as well as seven people from the EP Secretariat (two were in one interview); reaching near gender parity amongst the interviewees, and covering all seven political groups as well as non-attached MEPs (see Fig. 3.1).

Overview of Data

Across the two phases of data gathering, several types of data were collected: interview data, ethnographic data and documentary material. In total, the team interviewed 140 MEPs and staff; reaching gender parity amongst the interviewees and covering all eight political groups and the

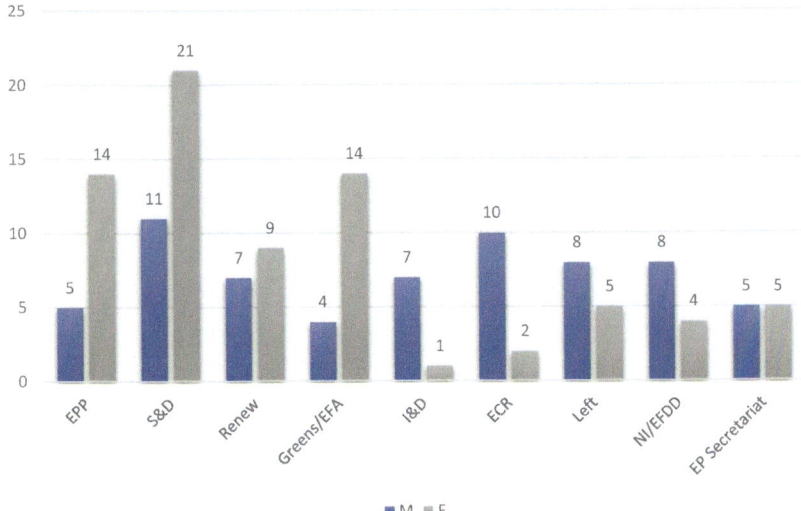

Fig. 3.1 Gender division of interviewees by political groups or secretariat

EP secretariat. At the same time, we conducted a parliamentary ethnography which included shadowing, participant observation, and fieldwork diaries. This was augmented with documentary and supplementary materials that the entire team collected for analysis (for more details see below sections). Quality and selection of the data often determine the qualitative outputs of research (cf. Gilgun, 2020). Since qualitative researchers seek to understand the subjective experiences of research participants in their contexts, high-quality data result in large part from the degree that researchers practise immersion and the degree that both researchers and informants develop rapport and engage with each other (as we discuss in further chapters) (Gilgun, 2020). Hence, we aimed to collect and often triangulate different types of data that would permit us to explore various facets of the studied political institution. This was particularly important since we aimed to shed light on the practices and informality with unequal power dynamics at play in the EP.

We did not achieve our planned numbers exactly (see Fig. 3.2), especially in terms of the division between MEPs and staff, but the material we collected was more than sufficient for analytical integrity (see Chapters 5 and 6).

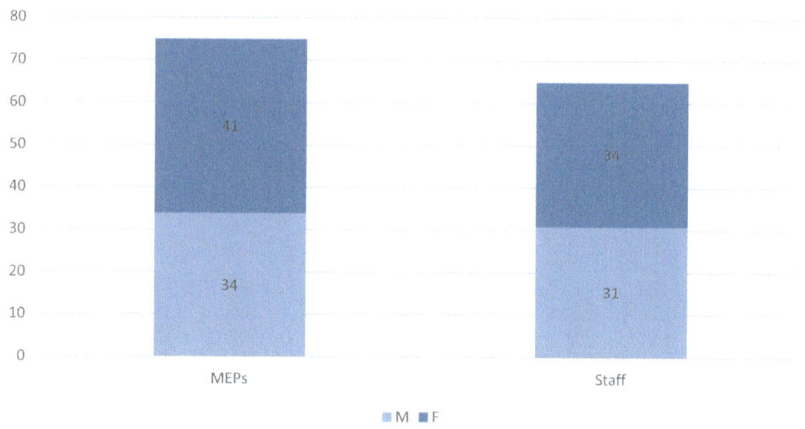

Fig. 3.2 Position of interviewees in the European Parliament

When divided by nationality, the interviewees revealed a correlation between the highest numbers of member state representatives in the EP and the EUGenDem team members' nationalities and spoken languages (see Fig. 3.3). The language skills of the researchers also had a clear impact on the numbers of interviewees who spoke English. The impact of language and nationality on data gathering will be considered in greater detail in Chapter 4, where our strategies for gaining access and obtaining interviews are more broadly elaborated. Suffice it to say, for smaller national delegations, it was more difficult to obtain interviews as there were fewer people to respond and those participants had greater demands on their time.

One of the main events to occur during the fieldwork in Brussels was the Brexit negotiations ultimately leading to the UK leaving the EU. These processes therefore became prominent in our research and led to several publications that were attentive to the various impacts of Brexit on the EP (see for instance, Gaweda et al., 2022; Kantola & Miller, 2022). Brexit had a clear impact on the numbers of most political groups in the EP (see Table 3.1.), and as a very salient issue, it also had a notable bearing on the numbers of UK nationals we interviewed.

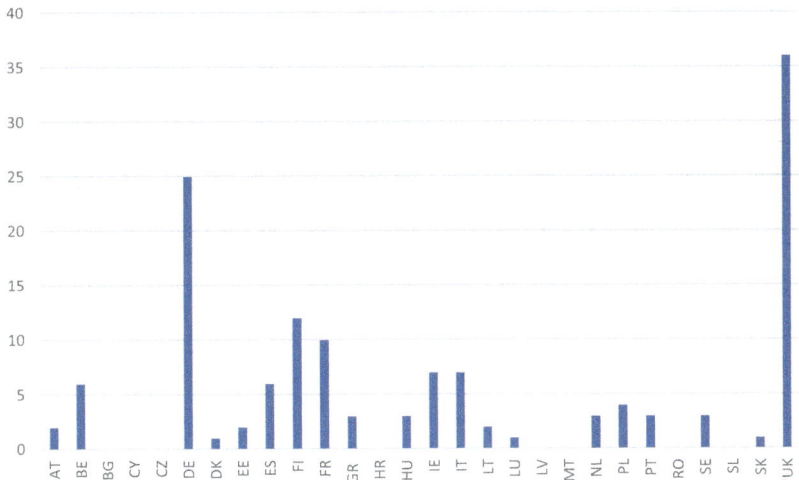

Fig. 3.3   Nationality of interviewees

Table 3.1   Seats lost by each political group after Brexit in 2020

Political group	73 seats from the UK
EPP	0
S&D	−10
Renew	−17
Greens/EFA	−11
I&D	0
ECR	−7
GUE/NGL	−1
NI	−27

Interview Data

Taken together, during the pilot and main data collection periods, we conducted 140 interviews with near gender parity and maintained a balance between MEPs and staff (see Table 3.2). The interviews covered the democratic practices of political groups, their leadership, MEP/staff lives, behaviour and conduct, and policy-making processes. The interviewees signed consent forms concerning data protection. Signing of forms became trickier at the beginning and during the restrictions related to

Table 3.2 Overview of the interviews

Political group	F MEP	M MEP	F Staff	M Staff	Total
EPP	10	4	4	1	19
S&D	10	7	11	4	32
ALDE/Renew	4	2	5	5	16
Greens/EFA	8	2	6	2	18
Left	2	2	3	6	13
ECR	2	7	0	3	12
EFDD/NI	4	6	0	2	12
ENF/ID	1	4	0	3	8
EP Secretariat	–	–	5	5	10
Total	41	34	34	31	140

the Covid-19 pandemic. In response, we accepted phone photographs of signed forms from our participants.

Ten per cent of interview participants were from racialised minorities: six MEPs (two women, four men); five group staff (two women, three men) and one parliamentary staff member (woman). Two MEPs from racialised minorities were shadowed—one woman and one man. We consciously avoid giving further information, for example, naming the political groups, so as not to compromise the anonymity of the participants, especially those from smaller political groups where there are fewer racialised minority MEPs and staff.

Post-Interview Notes

One of the additions we made following the pilot study was to take structured notes of our 'fresh' impressions immediately after the interviews. The post-interview note focused on three facets of the interview: the socio-spatial–temporal aspects; the interpersonal and affective relations; and any practical implications arising from the interviews. Each section included prompt questions that helped us reflect (see Fig. 3.4). We designed the post-interview notes as types of research diary entries that allowed us to record impressions, feelings and immediate reactions after the interview. They were also often a way of 'dealing' with more difficult situations or problematic statements from our participants, since the notes were accessible to all team members for reference. The post-interview notes had also the practical application of recording potential follow-ups and snowballing options that could otherwise be forgotten or missed in bilateral communications between team members. Due to time constraints and the fact that interviews were often planned back-to-back because of our participants' schedules, we managed to write up 36 post-interview notes for 79 interviews conducted in the main data collection period (a completion rate of about 45%).

Socio-Spatial-Temporal

- Where did they choose to have the interview?
- How long were you kept waiting? Was the meeting rushed or easy-going?
- What were they wearing?
- What is the office like: how is it occupied, are there pictures?
- What was the office set up - who sat where?

Human Relations/ Affect/ Positionality

- What was the mood of the participant, and how were their interactions with others?
- How did the persons make you feel during and after the interview? How did they relate to you? What was your subject position as a researcher? Did you experience or observe gender, age, class, etc. hierarchies?
- Was there a point in the interview where the participant became particularly animated?
- What were the power hierarchies in the office? Who fetched the tea/documents etc.
- Has your attitude towards the participant or the group changed as a result of the interview?

Implications for further research

- What would you ask the MEP/Staff member if you could conduct an interview with them again?
- Are there any follow-ups from the interview? Did they promise contacts/documents/further meetings?
- Did they suggest any names for you to contact?

Fig. 3.4   Post-interview note template

Ethnographic Data

Parliamentary ethnography was our main methodological innovation. It allowed us to gain a finer-grained understanding of (in)formal political group dynamics that otherwise would have been hard to reveal. In total, we shadowed nine MEPs and had access to ten political group meetings. During the main data collection period, our team member Dr. Cherry Miller secured a two-month placement at the European Parliamentary Research Service, which allowed by-appointment targeted observations of political groups, as well as other activities in the EP. Overall, this amounted to 55 days (or 440 hours) in the field. In terms of recording the data, our progressive focus on the 9th Parliament consisted of pioneering a five-concept observation protocol alongside a fieldwork diary (see Fig. 3.5). In total, we uploaded 193 pages of fieldnotes to ATLAS.ti (Computer Assisted Qualitative Data Analysis Software) and coded as a team (for details, see Chapter 5). Due to Covid-19, some of the observational activity in the latter part of the fieldwork was cancelled due to restrictions on meetings for both staff and visitors in the parliament. Covid-19 restrictions were disappointing, but the wealth and breadth of the already collected data allowed for the deeper analysis and wider research into overarching topics and themes that we wanted.

There are several ways to record parliamentary fieldnotes. Bussell (2020: 471), for example, suggests more structured forms of note-taking, structuring fieldnotes chronologically around a unit of observation, such as a column for time. In this sense, researchers take detailed field notes after every relevant fieldwork event (e.g. meeting, phone call conversation, informal chat, etc.). One such moment was after being approached by a member of the parliamentary administration who had moved from a political group and had a 'gripe' session. Whilst some ethnographers, faithfully record everything that happened in the meeting, we wished to be 'as inconspicuous as possible' (Mykkanen, 2001) and as a rule did not record meetings. One exception was a surprising invitation from the accredited parliamentary assistant of an EFDD group meeting, to openly record the proceedings. Such a material offer of using a Dictaphone potentially demonstrated that Dr. Miller had acquired a presence in the field as a *qualitative social researcher* (Laube, 2021).

Similarly to Mykkanen's (2001) observations of the Centre Parliamentary Party in the Finnish Parliament, during the pilot study our team members kept a running log of the meetings by hand. Despite not being

Event setting
*Date, *Duration, *Location, *Organizers, *PGs represented, *External visitors yes/no, * # to follow on Twitter, *MEPs/Staff in attendance

Power relations
*Hierarchy, *Interactions, * Leadership, *Seating arrangements

Democracy
*Information-sharing, *(Non) decision-making, *Speaking Time, *Representation, *Transparency

Gendered practices (considered intersectionally)
*Division of labour, *Gendered language/ humour, *Valuing expertise, *Embodiment, *Des Rep.

The Political Group as a Workplace
*Attendance, *Responsibilities, *Skills and trainings, *Collaborations, *Rules

Affect
*Moments of arousal/intensity/ (dis) engagement *Socio-material environment, *Strong language

Researcher role
*Own views, *Reactions, *Comments, *Affects, *Positionality

Fig. 3.5 Ethnographic observation protocol template

verbatim reports, they were as faithful to the words of the participants as possible. Quotation marks that were placed around certain words certainly were verbatim. During the pilot stage of data collection, there was no real unit of observation because the coding framework had yet to be devised, and given that our research was primarily interpretive, we were able to find the precise empirical focus iteratively. Therefore, the observations remained holistic and chronological.

During the main data collection, we developed a systematic observation protocol based on a structured form divided into seven sections. The sections were driven by Feminist Institutionalist conceptual lenses:

event setting (to convey the role of context, such as which attendees were in the room), power relations, democracy, gendered practices, the political group as a workplace, affect and researcher role. Counter to more positivist methods that might be more categorical for aggregating data statistically, our ethnographic notes were more descriptive and subjective (see Fig. 3.5).

Since one researcher was conducting all the ethnographic fieldwork, we implemented a practice of a weekly phone conversation between Brussels and Helsinki taking place every Friday. Instituting a set of debriefing practices with a supervisor or colleague is related to recording data. This may involve sending fieldnotes, observation protocols or an overview of activities attended that week to a peer for comments and discussion. Debriefing also occurred in the process of presenting findings and ideas at conferences, as well as to participants in the field, for example, to informal staff groups, in ways that ensured anonymity and confidentiality.

This section has been attentive to some of the practices and techniques useful for the recording of parliamentary ethnography. In our experience, there were many research questions organised around phenomena in parliaments that made ethnography a rich and fruitful methodology. Amongst other things, we discussed and shed light on, the nature of organisational change, new political and parliamentary contexts, such as new country accessions and democratic experiments like Spitzenkandidaten, new forms of (feminist) leadership, elections, conflict and contestation; all of which will be considered in greater detail in the following chapter.

Document Archive

Our team collected a wealth of internal documents from the EP and those covering the practices and policies of the political groups, consistent with fieldwork using ethnographic observations and interviews. These not only fed into the context and interview analysis but were also crucial in our publications (see, e.g. Ahrens & Kantola, 2022; Elomäki & Ahrens, 2022; Elomäki & Gaweda, 2022; Kantola et al., 2023).

Formal Political Group and EP Documents

The documents we collected included all the political group statutes which were either accessible online or after we had requested them from their staff by email (see Table 3.3). This did not include the documents of groups like the Left, because they do not have formalised statues. We gathered the statutes of all groups largely through our contacts, using direct means. In this way, we were able to access documents that were not available otherwise, such as internal guidelines, internal gender action plans and documents related to procedures on harassment. Documents that relate to the internal activities of the political groups are usually not publicly available, with only some publishing their statutes freely online (e.g. Greens/EFA, EPP, ID). Statutes govern the formal rules of the groups and were important to us as we published articles on their internal working practices.

Position papers and press releases on specific issues that groups often published on their websites were also collated. Political groups tend to share their positions more openly in press releases rather than during the policy process because decision-making in the EP is consensus-oriented. We collected the internal documents, position papers and press releases, as well as EP documents (EP rules of procedure that govern the organisation and function of the Parliament with relation to policy-making) and published debates. Access to these textual documents varied by political group. Some groups updated their websites and social media frequently, whilst others only posted occasional or topical content. Each type of document had a different role in the research and they complemented each other and the interviews. Most of our document archive was compiled for the purposes of individual articles, without shared data collection guidelines. For example, besides using the interview and ethnography dataset, Gaweda et al. (2022) collected national party electoral manifestos, as well as political group electoral programmes from the 2014 and 2019 EP elections for their study of the conservative ideology in the ECR group.

Policy-Related Documents

Beyond interviews, our data consisted of text derived from policy documents to which we applied content analysis. Amongst other things, reading documents about parliamentary work helps researchers familiarise themselves with policy narratives and their development across time (Prior, 2020). We discuss in greater detail how we analysed the documents in Chapter 6; however, here we want to discuss what was collected. We took a broad understanding of policy documents as any written

Table 3.3 Overview of official documents collected on political groups

	8th Parliamentary term	9th Parliamentary term
EPP	EPP group rules of procedure 2013 (amended in 2021)	
S&D	S&D Rules of procedure 2014	
ALDE/Renew	ALDE group rules of procedure 2009	Renew Europe rules of procedure 2022
Greens/EFA	Greens-EFA Statutes 2009	
ENF/ID	ENF Statutes 2015	ID Statutes 2019
ECR	ECR Constitution (amended in 2014 and 2017)	
GUE-NGL/Left	n/a	
EFDD	EFDD statutes (updated 2017)	n/a

records about EP policies and activities, which were gathered on a case-by-case basis, dependent on the research articles we were working on. These included transcripts of plenary debates, committee meeting videos and adopted legislative and non-legislative resolutions of the EP, along with draft report and committee and plenary amendments. For instance, Ahrens et al. (2022) produced an in-depth analysis of nine plenary debates dedicated to questions of human rights, gender equality and religious issues in addition to relevant interviews and ethnographic materials from the project dataset.

We analysed the economic policies of the political groups (e.g. Elomäki, 2021; Elomäki & Gaweda, 2022), next to interview data, through a dataset composed of non-legislative reports on the European Semester drafted by the Economic and Monetary Affairs Committee (ECON), and the Employment and Social Affairs Committee (EMPL). The dataset included draft reports, amendments, adopted texts and committee and plenary speeches and allowed the identification of differences between the political groups and committees in terms of constructions of gender equality, constructions of the social/economic relationship and specific social issues and economic ideas underpinning policy proposals.

Regarding policy tracing, we typically gathered draft reports or proposals, the amendments submitted by groups and MEPs in the relevant committee with appended explanations, the adopted committee reports, the last amendments submitted at the plenary stage and the final text adopted in plenary with the explanations of votes. These followed the journey of policy adoption, from committee negotiations to plenary vote (Ringe, 2010). Whilst the draft report reflects the views of the rapporteur and its political group, the amendments reflect the views of other political groups and MEPs sitting in the same committee. The latter shed light on the diverging priorities and contestations amongst, and within, the political groups. Once a compromise is reached at committee level, a report is adopted and may move to the plenary level where more amendments can be made. These documents are publicly available on the EP website as part of its commitment to transparency and can be easily found via a keyword search on the Public Register of Documents website of the EP. For each legislative and non-legislative process, the EP keeps records of all policy documentation on its 'Legislative Observatory' website.

We also gathered published records of debates at the committee level and plenary level. Unlike many other parliaments, the EP committee meetings are open to the public and video recordings are openly available on the EP website. These are important to study because they indicate the priorities of the political groups and if they support the view presented by the rapporteurs. The plenary is the most important deliberative space of the parliament, it provides the political groups and MEPs a forum for public attention and for sending messages to their constituencies (Brack, 2018; Kantola & Lombardo, 2021). Plenary debates are mainly performative, as a negotiated text already exists.

Plenary debates can also be found on the EP Public Register of Documents with a simple keyword search. One particularity of the European Parliament as a research context is that it has 24 official languages and MEPs often use their native language in the debates. Video recordings are available in the original multilingual form, as well as simultaneously translated into all official languages. For the plenary debates, the EP publishes written reports of all speeches in a multilingual form. For the committee debates, we relied on simultaneous English interpretation, when our own language skills fell short. For the plenary debates, we either used the English simultaneous interpretation or translated the native language speeches.

Debates complemented amendments and interview data as they highlighted contested and polarising issues. We found these kinds of debates to be revealing about the core positions of the groups and the views of individual MEPs, bringing out the tensions within the groups (Ahrens et al., 2022). When the purpose was to analyse strategies of opposition to gender equality (Kantola & Lombardo, 2021) or contestation of women's and LGBTQI rights (Ahrens et al., 2022), debates were selected to cover those that illustrated the greater level of contestation (i.e. convenience sampling). Such a strategy does not aim at generalising according to incidence and prevalence criteria (Soss et al., 2006: 136; Weiss, 1994), but rather to highlight the interpretative accounts of the group and MEPs regarding their strategies and discourses (Kantola & Lombardo, 2021; Yanow, 2006: 9)—core to our research questions (for more on the replicability of qualitative research see Ritchie et al., 2013; Seale, 1999). Finally, we did not approach debates by paying attention to gestures, tone, facial expressions and physical environment but rather as a written text channelling a political discourse (see for instance, Holm, 2020 for visual methods).

DATA STORAGE AND ARCHIVING

As previously noted, all interviews were recorded (if the participant agreed) and all data (including notes and transcripts) were stored on the protected drive of the host university. Following the pilot study, we decided to name all our files according to a jointly established system. First, the data files were sorted into the following five categories: MEP, APA, SG, PG staff, and PRESS. Then, all file names followed the prefix format: GROUP; POSITION; GENDER; DATE of interview (sometimes we included a NUMBER, if there were more than one interview within the same group on a given day). In addition, all ethnographic field note file names ended in _FN and post-interview notes in _IN. We also created several 'metadata' lists and tables that included information on nationalities, genders and the specific position of the interviewees.

A local transcription company recommended by the university completed all the transcriptions of Finnish and English interviews. One team member anonymised and uploaded the transcripts, submitted all the recordings and kept track of the ongoing cataloguing and archiving of data. This made the process more reliable and the cataloguing more consistent. Individual interviewers arranged transcriptions of interviews in French, German and Polish from national transcription services on a case-by-case basis.

During the pilot study, we attempted to translate some French interviews into English so that all team members could access them equally for analysis, but the quality was unsatisfactory and we felt that a lot of the nuance was lost in translation. For that reason, we transcribed, stored and later coded the interviews in their original languages, still maintaining the same cataloguing system (just adding language suffixes to name files, e.g. _pl for Polish or _de for German).

CONCLUSION: QUALITATIVE ASSESSMENT OF THE DATA

This chapter presented a thorough overview of the various types of data collected in the research project, including a description of our interviews (including post-interview notes), ethnographic field notes and the wide range of document data related to the EP and its political groups that we collated. Whilst we sought to undertake 170 interviews when designing the data-gathering period, we managed to get 140 interviews (still maintaining a gender balance in the dataset). Despite not reaching the numbers we expected, we were more than satisfied with the quality and content of the data, which provided us with a considerable tranche of material for analysis. The following chapter will cover in greater detail the logistical challenges we faced, suffice to say, 'objective' obstacles aside (e.g. the Covid-19 pandemic) the scheduling, rescheduling and 'juggling' of numerous interviews within weeks, and sometimes days, proved challenging. It imposed greater limits on our research than we would have liked.

In retrospect, our major takeaway from handling the data might seem trivial, but proved to be essential—we learned the hard way the importance of keeping track of the data and the locations of the files. Only after the pilot study were we forced to rethink and adapt older files; later we developed our archiving and labelling system for data files which was time well spent. Since we had files in various formats (audio, video, text, etc.), we needed a system that enabled us to be in control of their numbers and names, as well as our protocols for archiving, whilst maintaining participant anonymity and privacy. The sheer volume of data coming in during fieldwork would have been challenging to keep track of, had we not systematically maintained and regularly updated lists and tables of data files with information on gender, nationality, and positions in the EP. Concomitantly, writing up post-interview notes and ethnographic field notes proved easiest and most effective immediately after the events or interviews, despite the time constraints imposed by continuing fieldwork.

References

Ahrens, P., Gaweda, B., & Kantola, J. (2022). Reframing the language of human rights? Political group contestations on women's and LGBTQI rights in European Parliament debates. *Journal of European Integration, 44*(6), 803–819.

Ahrens, P., & Kantola, J. (2022). Political group formation in the European Parliament: Negotiating democracy and gender. *Party Politics*. Advance online publication. https://doi.org/10.1177/13540688221106295

Brack, N. (2018). Euroscepticism in the European Parliament. In N. Brack (Ed.), *Opposing Europe in the European Parliament: Rebels and radicals in the chamber* (pp. 51–81). Palgrave Macmillan.

Bussell, J. (2020). Shadowing as a tool for studying political elites. *Political Analysis, 28*(4), 469–486.

Elomäki, A. (2021). "It's a total no-no": The strategic silence about gender in the European Parliament's economic governance policies. *International Political Science Review*. Advance online publication. https://doi.org/10.1177/0192512120978329

Elomäki, A., & Ahrens, P. (2022). Contested gender mainstreaming in the European Parliament. *European Journal of Gender and Politics, 5*(3), 322–340.

Elomäki, A., & Gaweda, B. (2022). Looking for the 'Social' in the European Semester: The ambiguous 'Socialisation' of EU Economic Governance in the European Parliament. *Journal of Contemporary European Research, 18*(1), 166–183.

Gaweda, B., Siddi, M., & Miller, C. (2022). What's in a name? Gender equality and the European Conservatives and Reformists' group in the European Parliament. *Party Politics*. Advance online publication. https://doi.org/10.1177/13540688221116247

Gilgun, J. F. (2020). Writing up qualitative research. In P. Leavy (Eds.), *The Oxford handbook of qualitative research* (pp. 984–1011, 2nd ed.). Oxford University Press.

Holm, G. (2020). Photography as a research method. In P. Leavy (Ed.), *The Oxford handbook of qualitative research* (pp. 569–600). Oxford University Press.

Kantola, J., Elomäki, A., Gaweda, B., Miller, C., Ahrens, P., & Berthet, V. (2023). "It's like shouting to a brick wall": Normative whiteness and racism in the European Parliament. *American Political Science Review, 117*(1), 184–199.

Kantola, J., & Lombardo, E. (2021). Opposition strategies of right populists against gender equality in a polarized European Parliament. *International Political Science Review, 42*(5), 565–579.

Kantola, J., & Miller, C. (2022). Eternal friends or jubilant Brexiteers? The impact of Brexit on UK MEPs' parliamentary work in the European Parliament. *Journal of Common Market Studies*. Advance online publication. https://doi.org/10.1111/jcms.13424

Laube, S. (2021). Material practices of ethnographic presence. *Journal of Contemporary Ethnography, 50*(1), 57–76.

Leavy, P. (2020). Introduction to the Oxford handbook of qualitative research. In P. Leavy (Eds.), *The Oxford handbook of qualitative research* (pp. 1–20, 2nd ed.). Oxford University Press.

Mykkanen, J. (2001). Inside rationality: The division of labour in a parliamentary party group. *Journal of Legislative Studies, 7*(3), 92–121.

Prior, L. (2020). Content analysis. In P. Leavy (Ed.), *The Oxford handbook of qualitative research* (pp. 540–568, 2nd ed.). Oxford University Press.

Ringe, N. (2010). *Who decides, and how. Preferences, uncertainty, and policy choice in the European Parliament.* Oxford University Press.

Ritchie, J., Lewis, J., Nicholls, C. M., & Ormston, R. (2013). *Qualitative research practice: A guide for social science students and researchers*. Sage.

Seale, C. (1999). *The quality of qualitative research*. Sage.

Soss, J., Condon, M., Holleque, M., & Wichowsky, A. (2006). The illusion of technique: How method-driven research leads welfare scholarship astray. *Social Science Quarterly, 87*(4), 798–807.

Weiss, R. S. (1994). *Learning from strangers: The art and method of qualitative interview studies*. Free Press.

Yanow, D. (2006). Qualitative-interpretive methods in policy research. In F. Fischer, G. Miller, & M. Sidney (Eds.), *Handbook of public policy analysis* (pp. 405–415). Taylor & Francis.

CHAPTER 4

How Was the Data Gathered? Doing Research Interviews and Ethnography

Abstract The chapter describes the process of gathering data for research interviews and ethnography in the context of the European Parliament. First, the ethical review process is reviewed and discussed in light of the impact of the General Data Protection Regulation on interviews and ethnography. This chapter provides a detailed overview of how the interviews were conducted, outlines the selection and recruitment of interviewees and describes the preparatory steps ahead of the interview. It also offers various ethnographic practices that researchers can use in parliamentary research. Simultaneously, the chapter discusses the specificities of the research site that influenced data gathering. For example, in the European Parliament Strasbourg site, the long hours and close-knit community provided unique opportunities for building relationships and gaining credibility as 'insiders' through informal dialogues and shared experiences. However, the intense schedule and overlapping meetings made it challenging to secure interviews. Finally, the impact of Covid-19 on how the interviews were conducted and how the European Parliament operated, in general, is also discussed.

Keywords Data gathering · Interviewing practices · Ethnographic practices · Challenges · Covid-19

© The Author(s) 2023   51
V. Berthet et al., *Guide to Qualitative Research in Parliaments*,
https://doi.org/10.1007/978-3-031-39808-7_4

Introduction

How can contacts for elite interviews be established? How can interviews be secured with politicians when they are too busy to answer their emails? Which type of interview questions are likely to be effective for generating new knowledge and information? How can parliamentary ethnography be practically conducted? What needs to be considered in an ethics review for the undertaking of qualitative interviews and ethnography in a parliamentary environment? What are the specificities of interviewing parliamentarians and staff members in the multilingual context of the European Parliament?

This chapter addresses the above questions by focusing on how we gathered data through research interviews and ethnography in the context of the European Parliament. We draw on extant research employing qualitative methods, as well as our own experiences in conducting a large-scale qualitative study in the European Parliament. First, we provide insights into the meaning and practice of an ethical review in the context of researching the gendered practices and policies of the European Parliament's political groups. At its best, an ethical review can help researchers to clarify a number of practical issues, as well as ensuring that the research is ethically sound. Second, we discuss strategies for the selection of interviewees, strategies for contacting them and obtaining consent for the interviews. We go through the preparatory work required for securing elite interviews and outline our research interview questions and the choices we considered in drafting them. Third, we provide a practical overview of doing ethnography in parliaments. We show how we gained access to the research field, as well as providing a practical explanation of the ethnographic practices we used in the field.

Ethical Review

As with any research project, one of the very first steps was to undergo an ethical review with the funder (European Research Council) and with the host university (Tampere Region Ethics Council). Prior to the task of data gathering, this helped us clarify not just the ethical issues about how to proceed but also the practicalities of producing all the documents we needed for elite interviews and the parliamentary ethnography. Overall, the purpose of any ethical review is to protect the well-being of the research participants and to prevent abuses by scientists (Wasse-naar & Mamotte, 2012: 268–269). Importantly, ethical reviews ensure public trust in the integrity of the research process (Bond, 2012: 102). From the point of view of the ethics review, the first thing was to explain that the interviews with the Members of the European Parliament (MEPs) and parliamentary workers were elite interviews, considered as such because of their privileged position as politicians and workers within the European Parliament. We stated that the interviews were based on voluntary informed consent, confidentiality and anonymity. At the time of the initial contact, and prior to the actual interview, we outlined our commitment to a research procedure whereby the usage of the research data was anonymous, solely for the purposes of this project, its publications and wider dissemination. It was explained by the interviewer to the interviewee that the data would be stored securely and in line with recommended procedures.

In a multilingual setting such as the European Parliament, misunder-standings over language could compromise informed consent if not all the interviewees understood English. We made sure that the interviews we conducted in English were with participants who had high levels of spoken English and comprehension. In some cases, they asked to either see the interview questions beforehand or to bring a personal assistant or a colleague to assist with the interview in the event that clarification was required. These were of course allowed for. We also approached intervie-wees and conducted interviews in Finnish, French, German, Italian and Polish in which case the information was translated into these languages.

All interviewees were promised full anonymity. An informed consent form, which was signed by the interviewee and interviewer, detailed this issue, though this was only part of establishing informed consent. We have included the form as Appendix 1 as a reference for our project, but we are aware that different universities have their own procedures and templates with regards to ethics reviews. We also drafted the information sheet about the project, see Appendix 2, which detailed the purposes of the research, the conditions of full anonymity, that usage of the research data was solely for the purposes of this project, its publications and dissemination and the secure storage of participant observation notes.

We explained that interviews were to be recorded unless the inter-viewee requested otherwise, in which case notes would be taken. This arose in the actual interviews, where we had around 5 interviews out of 140 where we took notes instead. We clarified in the ethics review that interviews were to be conducted in public locations chosen by the interviewee or in their offices. The interviewees retained the right to withdraw from the interview process at any time, and to stipulate that the interview data was not to be used. The confidentiality criteria also included a statement that interview content was not to be discussed with any other participants. Given that the interviews might concern gender equality practices and informal institutions that could hinder or advance gender equality within the political groups, we were sensitive to matters of gender discrimination, racism or sexual harassment arising in the interviews (see, e.g. Muasya & Gatumu, 2013). All the interviewers would have information about the European Parliament's procedures for such cases, as well as contact details of relevant public or voluntary organisation support services which could be offered after the interview.

One of the trickiest ethical questions to address was how to acquire informed consent when carrying out a parliamentary ethnography. The first matter of note was that participant observation would occur in many locations, including plenary meetings of the European Parliament, different public events organised by the political groups, and public committee meetings. We explained that many of these, especially the plenaries and the committee meetings, were public events and as such were commonly televised or recorded. When undertaking participant observation in these places no personal data (e.g. names, nationality) was to be recorded.

The second measure was that we were committed to the principle that our research was to be conducted openly. The European Parliament was to be informed about the ongoing research and an information sheet was to be available to those chairing meetings and all participants. The researchers conducting the participant observation would also offer to discuss the purposes of the research project with the political groups and the committees. To that end, we undertook to organise an opening seminar in the European Parliament in Brussels to disseminate information about the ongoing project and our findings in the final stages of the research. We stated that an open approach to participant observation will also enhance the commitment of the institutions and actors in question. Subsequently, the opening and closing seminars were organised on 30 January 2019 and 7 February 2023, respectively, in the European Parliament in Brussels with the participation of our project researchers, other academics, our expert board members, MEPs and staff.

Thirdly, ethnographic research was also to be conducted in some closed meetings of the political groups or subgroups of the European Parliament. In such cases, we proposed the following procedure: the researcher would negotiate with the person in charge to obtain a permit to undertake participant observation, and amongst other things, explain the ethical principles followed in the research and make the information sheet available to all participants. The leader would inform the group about the ongoing research and the group could potentially discuss it. In such a way, everyone who participated in the meeting would have been informed, and nobody would have been under observation without knowing about the research.

Notwithstanding this comprehensive approach to ethics, full informed consent is difficult to meaningfully achieve in ethnographic research. Specifically, total anonymisation is difficult and if participants provide data on third parties, these third parties cannot give their consent. However, the opening project seminar allowed us to establish a *presence* as *social researchers* in the parliament, and to a large degree making the ethnographic research both noticeable and accessible to the participants (Laube, 2021). We also showed the ethnographic observation protocol on one occasion of seeking access to a political group meeting and shared interview research questions with participants in advance. Furthermore, informed consent was not regarded as a one-off agreement. As a project, we frequently reflected on how we could establish and sustain our presence as social researchers of the European Parliament. For example, we maintained an active Twitter account and a frequently updated project website.[1]

In addition to these project-specific ethical principles, we committed not to gather or record any personal data (e.g. names or identity traits) and to follow the duty of not harming participants (e.g. by disrupting political careers). We only kept track of aggregate data that was already publicly available (like nationality or gender) for our own records, and presented it in our publications in general 'meta' terms. We undertook to continually evaluate the risk of identification by removing any indirect identifiers (e.g. nationality, occupation, age) prior to the publication

[1] For further discussion of the entree and access in ethnography as an in situ way of gaining informed consent, see below.

of any citations. The ethics review also included a detailed data management plan that described how we would keep transcribed interviews and fieldnotes securely and confidentially on the university drive.

Overall, during the whole research process, we noted the increased importance given to ethical considerations, not just by funding bodies, such as the European Research Council, but also by some high-ranking academic journals, such as the American Political Science Review for whom we were required to submit a full overview, and statements of our ethics review, when our article was accepted for publication.

In recent years, academia has witnessed debates about whether strict ethics reviews are making qualitative research particularly difficult. For instance, Fouché and Chubb (2017) in their literature review on ethics reviews and research involving participants, demonstrated that the criteria used for ethical review have been slow to adapt to the emergent and participatory nature of this research. This has resulted in researchers reporting negative attitudes towards, and experiences with, review boards and ethics review processes. Social science researchers' negative experiences with ethical reviews can be attributed to 'time delays involved in obtaining ethics reviews' due to the infrequent convening of university ethics committees (Wassenaar & Mamotte, 2012: 271). Yet, as we have outlined above, there are strategies for managing the ethical review that can be utilised that we recommend in order to conduct participatory research in an ethical manner.

Finally, the EU General Data Protection Regulation (GDPR) which came into effect in May 2018, obligates any organisation who 'target' or collect data related to people in the EU to adhere to specific rules. Because the regulation is admittedly large, far-reaching, and fairly light on specifics, compliance with it can become a daunting prospect, the EU launched a dedicated portal with guidance on compliance (https:/ /gdpr.eu/). Since 2018, GDPR has had an impact on ethical questions for interview-based research or ethnography as well as the scope of scientific choices available to researchers. Within the context of the GDPR and the sensitive status of personal data, there is a concern that academics will increasingly restrict their research choices to safer options. This may involve, for example, reusing anonymised datasets, selecting populations based on expediency rather than theoretical appropriateness or outsourcing fieldwork to professional data collection companies (Molina & Borgatti, 2021: 13). Scholars argue that the social sciences are particularly vulnerable to the intersection of ethics reviews and personal data collection, given the methodologies involved in the research field (Molina & Borgatti, 2021: 13). Whilst the GDPR puts more demand on obtaining valid consent from research participants and is rooted in ethical principles to safeguard fundamental rights, Molina and Borgatti (2021: 18) call for the establishment of more specialised social science ethics committees to address these ethical dilemmas facing the social sciences in the new digital age. At the outset of our research, the GDPR was just beginning to be implemented and both researchers and universities were not yet aware of how to enact the requirements. In the subsequent years, most institutions have established rules and procedures regarding GDPR and participant research, making it necessary to add GDPR compliance as a step in a comprehensive ethics review.

In conclusion, there is a constant need to commit to high ethics standards, with a very clear picture of what research is actually planned, and to conduct research according 'to the rules' established and agreed on with participants at every stage of the process.

Doing Interviews

The clear, principled and relatively straightforward world of the ethics review confronts a messy reality when interviews and ethnography actually begins. This messy reality is marked with constant negotiations around getting agreements for interviews from and actually interviewing, very busy people who can sometimes dedicate only 15–20 minutes in the corridor, to a researcher who wants to talk to them in a silent office for at least an hour to cover all the important interview questions, whilst conforming to the ethics requirements (see Box 4.1).

The initial step prior to beginning the interviews is to imagine the sample—ideally, who do you want to interview and why? For us, it was primarily MEPs, across all genders, all political groups and from different member states that were the main interviewees. We also wanted to interview parliamentary staff who are employed within, and by political groups, which added scholarly and practical benefits to our work and strengthened our research findings. The insights from these interviewees significantly helped our conceptualisation and analysis of power relations, informal institutions and gendered norms. Moreover, we heard the voices of those who have 'less power', but might nonetheless exhibit less restraint in talking about what they have observed, vis-à-vis parliamentary relationships, more acutely and/or from a different angle. In scholarly terms, as we argued in Chapter 2, there is a real gap in researching parliamentary staff. We interviewed many Accredited Personal Assistants (APAs) of MEPs, of whom it may be argued, were the most vulnerable category in our research material. Two of our research topics—sexual harassment and racist practices within the parliament—would have very much benefited from research interviews with caterers, cleaners and care-takers in the parliament, who had, unfortunately, fallen outside of our planned interviews and the ethics review.

Secondly, we wanted to include interviewees from different hierarchical positions to get a full sense of the gendered relations and practices of the political groups. We were not concerned with how representative certain statements or views were, which would have involved counting very carefully the number of interviews, and by whom, in which such statements were made, and ensuring that the sample was representative (see Goplerud, 2021). Rather, we sought to establish the qualitative dimensions of issues such as informal decision-making institutions, which underpinned our interest in talking to people in different positions. The highest echelons of power in our interview data were represented by the leadership of the political groups and administrative leadership, namely, the (Vice) Secretary Generals. We also targeted people across committees and in different positions within them, including the powerful positions of chairs, coordinators, rapporteurs and shadow rapporteurs. In addition to the above, we also wanted to ensure that those we interviewed were of different ages and stages of their political careers.

Even though our research was about gender equality, it was important that we did not target only those MEPs and staff who had shown interest in, or commitment to, gender equality during their political or work careers. To be more precise, we wanted to interview 'everyone'— not just women or feminists—but also men, and those who were not interested in gender equality or even opposed it. For us, this was a way to go beyond the 'usual suspects' in gender and politics research, and to locate discourses and practices of gender equality within political groups (see also Elomäki & Ahrens, 2022). This was aided by the parliamentary ethnography that went beyond, and renewed, 'the usual' pool of participants in studies of parliaments.

We did, however, (with mixed success, see Box 4.1) want to target some key actors in the setting who would have a greater knowledge about gendered practices and policies than others. These included the coordinators of the political groups in the Committee on Gender Equality and Women's Rights (known as the FEMM Committee), political group staff working for the FEMM committee, as well as gender mainstreaming administrators from all committees. For the specific policy issues—economic policy, social rights pillar and violence policy—it was essential to interview MEPs and staff who were working on these topics, on relevant files or in relevant committees, to enhance our understanding of policy processes.

> **Box 4.1 Reflections Post-Interview with Actors Involved in Gender Equality**
>
> 'It was a corona interview and I had 20 minutes negotiated between appointments. (…) but because of this short time, it felt that the interview lacked a narrative to it as I had to keep jumping between topics to cover the specific policy questions. Some of her interview performance betrayed a confusion around the proliferation of different structures, initiatives, and actors dealing with gender mainstreaming, especially when she is a usual suspect to be part of the initiative—her staff member was present and reminded her which gender initiative it was and her (non)role in this case: "you were sat in the room with them, but not part of the meeting". It perhaps shows even more who conducts the labour of being a gender equality actor. Affects and researcher role—the role of laughter in inappropriate situations—finding ignorance of gender simultaneously bizarre and funny, but also serious—this reminds me of Hochschild's "feeling rules". Feminists are not supposed to find the dire situation of gender and institutions funny, but sometimes they do' (EUGenDem research diary 9 Apr 2020).

STRATEGIES FOR RECRUITING INTERVIEW PARTICIPANTS

Several recruitment strategies for qualitative research are developed in the literature including probability sampling, maximising range sample, comparison cases and so on (see Weiss, 1994 for more). We combined convenience sampling with snowballing.

For us, the recruitment of participants started with convenience sampling (Weiss, 1994). In our case, this meant reaching out to actors we identified as allies. We understood allies in a broad sense, as anyone we had already made contact with, anyone potentially interested in our research topic or anyone with a similar nationality to ours. In this regard, our feminist and European networks helped greatly. Many of our participants were recruited based on their expertise on a specific issue. For instance, when analysing a policy issue, we targeted MEPs that were members of the committee in charge of it (e.g. MEPs in the Committee on Economic and Monetary Affairs when analysing economic policies). Reaching out to MEPs for an interview by appealing to their expertise, triggers their interest and increases the chances of receiving an answer. This strategy demands necessary and 'ultra-important' (Lilleker, 2003) preparatory work to find such expertise and to learn about the participant's background.

Overall, across the four years the data collection took place, we contacted around 500 people, which resulted in the 140 interviews that formed the core part of our data. Over the course of sending the emails, we learnt the importance of mixing a short official style—including mentioning the funding body and the university affiliation—with some personal details. Personal hooks included stating the reasons why we contacted this person in particular: on someone else's recommendation (i.e. a colleague in the European Parliament) because they worked on a particular file (i.e. they were an expert) or they held a particular position we were interested to know more about (i.e. a leadership position). Because MEPs and staff are very busy, and not always physically present in the European Parliament's locations of Brussels and Strasbourg, it was important to mention that the interview could be arranged whenever, and wherever, they saw fit.

Some participants were also recruited by researchers with similar nationalities. Thanks to having a team of six researchers from five different nationalities (Finland, France, Germany, Poland, the UK), we used our respective nationalities strategically to recruit MEPs. In the supranational context of our research, appealing to regionality and local references helped in building connections with MEPs and thus in augmenting our response rate. We found it useful to stress regional similarities in our invitation emails, for instance, by mentioning attendance at the same schools/Universities or similar citizenship, which tends to be particularly decisive for small member states like Nordic or Baltic countries (e.g. by being Finnish). However, we found out that this strategy remains context specific. Whilst it worked well for the Nordic countries, it did not result in any success with Polish or French radical-right groups.

As seen in Fig. 3.3 in the previous chapter, we obtained the most interviews based on linguistic and citizenship affinities—we had a high number of British participants, but also Germans, and Finns. It was easier to obtain interviews with participants who spoke English, e.g. we had more Irish interviewees than we could have expected based on the proportion of parliamentarians relative to member states.

For some nationalities, it was not possible to do interviews in English. For example, many Polish or Greek speakers were unwilling or unable to answer in languages other than their own. Some potential interviewees were particularly hesitant because they did not speak English at all and the arrangements for potential translators or interpreters would be too much hassle. To counteract this, we offered to do interviews in participants' native languages whenever we could. The composition of our team meant that we could offer interviews in English, Finnish, German, French, Italian and Polish. When asked, we also provided the interview questions beforehand in the native language and we also provided a printed interview guide in a clear accessible format, for participants who wanted to read particular interview questions. We also had several experiences, with Italian participants who were happy for interviews to be conducted in English, with one participant's assistant boasting that the MEP could equally do the interview in Italian, English, Spanish or French. The language politics of the European Parliament suggest an elite English dimension to relationships within the institution context of the willingness and ability to use English structured along North–South and East–West lines (Ringe, 2022).

The above-mentioned convenience sampling strategies increased the likelihood of getting an answer and establishing entry points to the European Parliament. Thereafter, we continued with a *snowball sampling strategy* by asking for recommendations after each interview to expand our pool of participants (Weiss, 1994). However, as Weiss (1994: 29) pointed out, we were aware of the pitfalls of snowballing strategies, especially the potential to under-represent the experience of those with little or no social contacts or networks.

Not only did we write emails according to the expertise and nationality of potential participants, which in some cases meant translating the email, but we also had to deal with conservative/radical-right populist actors. For the latter, we emphasised 'equality' more broadly as a focus of our research about 'men and women in the European Parliament'— as opposed to 'gender', even though these terms did not always reflect the normative foundation of our research. Although we cannot expect policymakers or non-academics to understand theoretical distinctions between different terms, this choice sometimes felt like self-censorship or self-imposed restriction.

As a rule, if a participant was not available for an interview we would ask if they could recommend potential participants in the same way as we did at the end of an interview. Our post-interview note also had a section on follow-ups that included a request for information about possible interviewees or research materials. Beckmann and Hall (2013: 200) present a useful concept of 'informed probing' at the end of the interview stage by adopting a more direct approach if familiar names are volunteered, and asking more generally about adjacent participants, for example, 'what about potential participants in X field?'. According to them, this allows for the building of further connections with the next participant in the invitation email, which they refer to as a 'name-drop' to elicit 'toehold respondents' (Beckmann & Hall, 2013: 201).

Once emails are drafted and sent, there is no guarantee that they will be answered. Therefore, both patience and persistence were required. We followed up the interviews with phone calls. In the European Parliament, phone numbers are usually displayed on the MEPs' webpage, and assistants can be contacted by changing one digit only (e.g. a 5 becomes 7). Due to their busy schedules, some elite interview participants prefer to handle demand with rapidity. For example, as MEPs and their staff are highly sought-after by various actors (i.e. lobbyist, researchers, national policymakers, grassroot organisations), they may be more receptive to immediate phone call demands, rather than to emails that can be archived or are easily lost amongst the masses received every day. In addition, when in the parliament, we also used door knocking and simply approached parliamentary actors on the spot.

Because we sought the widest representation of participants in the European Parliament as possible, we developed an activity log in which we documented and kept records of whom we contacted and recruited. The log helped us to ensure our pool of participants reflected a gender balance and fairly represented the range of political views in the Parliament. Each contacted participant was thus registered in the log with information about their gender, associated political groups, and also the date of the first invitation emails sent as well as follow-up emails or phone calls. The log was a key element in the development of a successful recruiting strategy. In this regard, systematically followed up on invitations, shared the workload with members of the team and assigned tasks of contacting some participants to those familiar with specific languages. This log was stored completely separately from the coded data and the metadata, ensuring that no crossover or identification could be made.

Preparing for Interviews: Preparatory Work, Locations and Interview Questions

Elite interviews are often hard-won, short and resource-intensive (including the participants' time). Therefore, preparatory work for each participant is essential to know their parliamentary and work biography; policy expertise, voting record and public statements. This allows for smoother follow-up questions and ensures that the interview material is not a duplication of publicly available data. Targeted follow-up questions allows researchers to steer the conversation beyond 'pat answers' (Chappell, 2020). There can be some risks related to preparatory work, not least over-determining the interview; anticipating answers in advance and ventriloquising participants. It also has workload risks on scholars less acquainted with the fieldsite, its political developments and participants or on early career scholars who feel the need to make expertise visible in the interview (although the benefits of the naive, unthreatening researcher, may be overrated).

At times, the activities of the European Parliament can feel overwhelming. Actors are busy and constantly moving from one city to another. The calendar of the European Parliament, known to all in the 'Brussels bubble', gives important information about the organisational structure of the parliament and its activities. The calendar, released in advance each May and voted on in a plenary, has eleven plenary sessions that must be held in Strasbourg. The working months are divided into four weeks; a pink week for Committee work, a blue week for Group work, a red week for Plenary work and a green week for Constituencies (Busby, 2013: 99). Each Friday is reserved for constituency affairs. In that sense, MEPs are constantly expected to travel between constituencies, Brussels and Strasbourg—making their time 'a precious commodity' (Busby, 2013: 146) and the calendar an important tool for scheduling interviews. For the parliamentary ethnography we undertook, the weeks when MEPs were in their constituencies—if they were not on delegations—were a good time for conducting interviews with staff and online. Furthermore, the first green week in February was used to contact some UK members who had left the parliament, since the experience of Brexit was still fresh in their minds.

With regard to the locations of the interview, several issues had to be considered. We asked participants to propose a location that was both accessible and comfortable for them. This mattered especially with disabled participants where further accessibility requirements could be made such as sign language skills (Evans & Reher, 2022: 700). Many matters were considered when arranging interviews, such as guaranteeing anonymity, the opportunity to record, safety considerations regarding Covid, as well as practicalities like allowing for enough time to get through security.

Our interviews were semi-structured. Semi-structured questionnaires correspond to adopting a conversational format with open-ended questions for in-depth interviews (Soss, 2006). Compared to structured interviews, they allow some leeway to follow-up on whatever is deemed important by the researcher (Brinkmann, 2020). To guide the interviews we developed a joint interview guideline, which we revised after the pilot study and then again two years into the project to reflect new research agendas, such as the impact of the Covid-19 pandemic on the work of the MEPs and staff. Time with the interviewees was always constrained. Consequently, we dropped some interview questions that we felt were already covered, including sexual harassment, a topic on which we published early in the project (Berthet & Kantola, 2021). We had a separate interview guideline for MEPs and staff, and separate interview questions for the topic of Brexit and for specific policy fields, such as economic, social and violence policy.

We opened the interviews with a very short background question. Such questions are often considered important as they can warm up the interviewee, relax the interview situation and build trust. Initially, we had two rather general questions: '*In which positions, and for how long, have you worked in the European Parliament? Who and whose interests do you see yourself as representing in European level politics?*' After the pilot study, we quickly dropped these due to time constraints for us, and the amount of time it took the MEPs to answer these. Instead, we opened the interviews with a question that we thought took us directly to issues that would provide better insights into our research questions: '*If you were to advise a new MEP on how to be an effective MEP in your political group, what would you stress? What's important to understand about the group?*'. For us, these questions provided insights about the informal institutions and hidden power structures of the political groups.

Our initial interview guideline included well-balanced parts, and the questions evolved over the course of the project and as our own knowledge increased they became more focused. For example, we dropped a whole section dealing with national politics and elections as we realised that this was not providing insight to our research questions. Instead, most interviews became focused in a very detailed way on the political group level, where insights on the democratic functioning of the political groups in terms of gender equality could be acquired. By the end, we had reduced the interview questions to practically one part relating to this.

When we asked about the MEPs' everyday involvement with the political group, we were attentive to their descriptions of decision-making in the political group; what they thought makes an effective group leader and whether gender played any role in this. We also asked about the significance of the political group meeting for the interviewee and the relations the MEP had to the group leader, the Secretary General, to other MEPs and staff. Our specific questions about gender equality followed these questions and were formulated as: '*How would you describe your political group from the point of view of gender equality more generally? What other differences are important?*' and '*What kind of practices for gender equality do you have within the party group?* (quotas, work-life-balance, etc.)'. The question alluding to 'what other differences are important' was designed to seek insights about other bases of inequality than gender, including race and ethnicity, disability or sexual orientation. We were interested in asking the question openly to see what basis of inequality the interviewees would see as most relevant. However, on reflection, we did think that we should have guided the interview more strongly in relation to intersectionality and inequalities other than gender, including racism (see, e.g. Kantola et al., 2023).

We had specific interview questions about policy-making in the political groups which included: '*How does policy-making work in your group? What are your possibilities for influencing group priorities and policies? Have you actively put yourself forward to some positions and failed/succeeded? What had an impact on your success/failure? How do you persuade people within the group, to whom do you go?*' We also asked about conflict and informal socialising within the political groups—always including the question of whether gender played a role in either. We also asked about the MEP's working relationships with other political groups and any obstructive behaviour between them. In addition to these policy-related questions, we asked about speaking in the plenary, and what made this effective, or conversely, hampered it. To complement these, we had a list of specific questions about the impact of Covid-19 on MEPs and political group work on Brexit, Europarties, codes of conduct and sexual harassment within the groups.

With these questions and follow-up enquiries, we were tapping into the practices and informal institutions of the political groups: how they worked in relation to power; informal politics; norms; practices; gender. One of our findings revealed that it was not easy for many intervie-wees to talk about such matters, whilst discussing specific policies and policy content came more easily and far more naturally to them. This relates to several important points for research: gendered hierarchies and informal institutions are difficult to study because they are invisible and embedded in the very power structures which are difficult to perceive and to talk about. Parliamentarians are generally concerned about being re-elected, which is realised on the basis of the policy work that they do, not for making their political groups or parliaments work better and in a more democratic way. This is also where the value of qualitative research reveals itself most intuitively: gathering a data set of qualitative interviews where several interviewees try to talk about the same topic, will generate multiple qualitative insights about things that are difficult to talk about for individual interviewees.

This ought not obscure the fact that elite interviews present many chal-lenges. Beyond those related to recruiting participants, scholars pointed to the difficulties of accessing knowledge during interviews with polit-ical elites (Holmes et al., 2019). Many discussed the power dynamics at stake between the interviewer and the political interviewee. This includes, for instance, the possibility of receiving a 'political talk' since 'politicians are used to evading difficult questions' (Cowley, 2021: 3). Katharine

Sarikakis convincingly shows that even if the researcher asks the questions, a reversal of power hierarchy can function between the researcher and the participants (2003: 423). In our case, such reversal occurred when participants asked us, for instance, to define concepts like racism. Another challenge includes the lack of trust between interviewee and interviewer during 'fly in fly out' interviews (Chappell, 2020: 135) that only ethnographic methods can provide a balance (Brown, 2018; Miller, 2022).

Doing fieldwork requires much data management and paperwork for both the researcher and the participant. Not only signing the consent form but also carrying around confidential paperwork. Efficiency is key, otherwise, it can put additional burdens on participants. There can be problems if participants do not sign the consent form immediately, which creates considerable additional work to print, sign and scan. In order to keep all of this safe and anonymous, we scanned consent forms to the server and then destroyed their hard copies.

SOME ADDITIONAL HURDLES: 'STRESSBOURG' AND COVID-19

Strasbourg provided both an opportunity and a challenge for conducting qualitative research. In terms of opportunities, the long hours and informal community in Strasbourg created opportunities for dialogue in the margins of meetings and spaces to build rapport. The change in atmosphere is palpable and the culture is more contained. Parliamentary actors all stayed in hotels, rather than returning home, were more dressed up, drank Crément d'Alsace, and frequented bars and restaurants and thus there were plenty of opportunities to speak and develop a rapport in a distinct way. Arguably, we gained greater credibility as an 'insider' at the margins of meetings, and in the practice of travelling to Strasbourg alongside political group staff, interpreters and members of the parliamentary administration in a carpool. Moreover, in Strasbourg, political group meetings are held in the evenings, rather than in the morning or in the afternoon in Brussels, which creates later days and a different atmosphere. Political group leaders' press conferences are all held in Strasbourg and are open to attend.

Strasbourg also provides its own distinct challenges. Busby (2013: 99), for example, has noted how some assistants referred to the Strasbourg week as 'Stressbourg', reflecting the long hours and hectic schedules.

Assistants would often not schedule interviews with themselves, or with MEPs, for that week because many pre-booked meetings would be running simultaneously, such as with lobbyists, group meetings or the plenary. To counter this, we were able to do ethnography in a political group meeting. Helped by a senior contact, we were able to attend a political group meeting organised by the Left Group (also known as GUE/ NGL), which was not recorded and published online, but was marginally more accessible than other political group meetings (Miller, 2022).

Brussels, by contrast, provided very different experiences. Some less active MEPs, or those who were not in positions of seniority in their political groups, were reluctant to host researchers, saying 'there's not much on this week', for example, during some committee weeks.

Whilst the fieldwork was multi-sited in Brussels and Strasbourg, the geographically dispersed and transnational nature of the MEPs, meant that they were often present in national capitals and cities of team members who could approach them for interviews. For example, the Left Groups (also known as GUE/NGL) held their study days in Helsinki, whilst some of our interviews were conducted in London and Berlin depending on the locations of both the MEPs and our team researchers. After the onset of Covid-19, this changed yet again, and our telephone and online interviews were conducted with participants either at home or in their 'local' offices in member states.

Like every aspect of normal daily activities, our data collection endeavour was equally transformed by the Covid-19 pandemic and accompanying restrictions. Due to the latter affecting parliamentary activities and access to the Parliament, we had to modify our recruitment and interview strategies. A major impact on our data collection was the closing of the Parliament as a whole, which by definition ended the ethnography.

When the Covid pandemic had just begun, various changes impacted our activities. The status of the Visitor's pass became ambiguous, and clarification had to be continuously sought about its status. Project resources and data collection very quickly had to be balanced against safety for others in the parliament as well as for the researchers. In the earliest days, events were attended, such as a Press Conference given by David Sassoli, then President of the European Parliament, about the openness of the parliament who alluded to how the key democratic functions of the institution would be retained. Eventually, however, meetings became closed to everyone except MEPs, and interviews were conducted in person and then eventually online, or by telephone call. Exceptionally, the parliamentary calendar was updated and trips to Strasbourg were cancelled. This meant that travel arrangements had to be undone at the last minute, and our 'exit' from the ethnography was unconventional, not least because traditional thanks could not be given, but also due to the field site itself, which became inaccessible to its members who had moved their work online.

As a project, we were forced to reassess our logistics and switch to online and phone call interviews. This generated advantages and disadvantages. Amongst the advantages, online and phone call interviews allowed for acting spontaneously and quickly, instead of limiting the schedule to when the researcher is visiting the location (in our case, Brussels and Strasbourg). These interviews are also easier to record and the presence of the dictaphone is less obvious. However, amongst the disadvantages, the interviewee can end meetings more easily, either due to bad connections (real or imagined) or to distraction from homeschooled children. In addition, these interviews create a distance which makes it more difficult to build a connection, to create a normal conversation or to observe body language. A further practical disadvantage is the difficulty to get consent forms signed and returned.

In relation to plenary debates, the Covid-19 pandemic significantly changed the setting, with debates being conducted within a hybrid format. In these circumstances, only a few MEPs were present in the European Parliament, and most contributed from their homes in Brussels or in their home countries. It was quite odd to see the MEPs in relaxed clothing, in their living rooms or separate office rooms, even in their kitchens.

DOING ETHNOGRAPHY

Ethnographic research within parliaments offers many advantages in the exploration of how the functions of parliaments are entangled (Crewe, 2021), especially the symbolic dimensions of parliaments such as their architectures (Verge, 2022: 1053), and how political work is differently carried out (Crewe, 2015). Ethnography reveals multiple interpretations of the same event or process, such as parliamentary work at the time of Brexit (Kantola & Miller, 2022); institutional hierarchies (Lewicki, 2017); how working worlds in parliaments are reproduced through everyday gendered relations (Miller, 2021) and what concepts such as gender,

gender hierarchies, gendered relations and their redress *mean* in and for everyday lives in parliamentary settings (Miller, 2022). This short section shows how ethnography may be fruitfully done in one parliament. Other parliaments may differ: some are far smaller, which makes some practices more difficult, since the researcher might become more visible and collaborations with other parties might be more visible, whilst others may be larger, making a finer-grained analysis more complex.

As discussed above, our research design consisted of a pilot study to shadow nine MEPs from five political groups and a longer stay as a study visitor. This ethnography took an explicitly political focus, centring on activities, rules and practices of the political groups of the European Parliament in the so-called 8th and 9th Parliaments (the legislatures of 2014–2019 and 2019–2023). Whilst an interpretative approach was taken to the European Parliament (Geddes & Rhodes, 2018; Miller, 2021), 'aspects of power central to politics, such as competition, conflict and interests' (Firat, 2019: 16) were also attended to.

Here we present some strategies and tradeoffs for those wishing to produce ethnographic data on parliaments. First, there are different entry routes into parliaments where permission needs to be sought to conduct research. It should be noted that a parliament is not a unified entity, they consist of many different actors with different jurisdictions, and so any permission to enter needs to be reflexively considered, especially with regard to issues of informed consent. One entry route we used was the two-month European Parliamentary Research Service placement. This was good for establishing a base to make contacts and request attendance at meetings, though access through this route provides no guarantee of gaining a presence in the myriad political worlds of parliament (Niemi, 2010: 107–113). Prior to the placement, the researcher can use personal and academic networks to identify participants who might be able to cooperate with the research and request to attend meetings.

Another route is through parliamentary leadership, political leadership or administrative leadership. In the European Parliament, this would be through the President, Vice-President, Bureau; political group leaders and the Secretary Generals of Political Groups. We did attempt this, although it proved to be our least successful strategy for several reasons. The Parliamentary and political leadership is likely to be more defensive in order to preserve the reputation of 'the good institution'. We quickly found out that trying to negotiate access at this level involves a meeting, the production of materials (beyond the information sheet) and an explanation of what the research is interested in. There may also be reciprocal responsibilities tied to such an opening, for example, presenting a final report or giving evidence to a committee. Entry through the parliamentary leadership may deliver cooperative benefits, but when feeding back research findings to different groups in the hierarchy, field members might feel they are being watched by the parliamentary leadership, leaving researchers in the role of reinforcing hierarchical structures of control. Finally, there is the inherent risk of institutional patronage: these leaderships might change and concomitantly jeopardise the continuation of the research.

The third, and the most effective point of entry for us, was through individual MEPs' offices. Here, an MEP might share their calendar and find a time in the placement for an interview. Gaining access with an MEP might be more successful (in our case) if they are a feminist MEP, have a shared policy interest or have expressed an attitude or experience in public sympathetic to the research project. Strategic positionality (Reyes, 2018) matters here, and the nature of what will be 'strategic' will vary by parliaments. As discussed above, nationality and language played a significant role in the European Parliament, meaning a multilingual team was advantageous in negotiating access. Political party activism and regional links also helped.

Persistence with contacting the relevant office was important, and so too was stressing our flexibility. One MEP wanted to cancel a shadowing placement on the same day that we were flying to Brussels, due to the fact that there was 'not much interesting' happening. This was potentially problematic because we did not have access via the European Parliamentary Research Service at the time, and thus a significant part of the trip would be cancelled and resources wasted. In the end, we emphasised how we were interested in observing all aspects of the parliamentary calendar and that we would be able to use the opportunity to conduct interviews. Luckily, we also had a shadowing placement scheduled later on that week. The lesson learned was to make sure we scheduled multiple activities whilst in Brussels. It is fortuitous for those seeking to conduct parliamentary ethnographies, that MEPs hire several assistants. This can increase the capacity for hosting a parliamentary shadowing placement, though inevitably places strains on staff working days. In smaller parliaments (Niemi, 2010: 105), this opportunity is squeezed as parliamentarians have smaller staffing budgets with which to employ multiple assistants.

Arguably, the key to entry is transparency. Formally, the information sheet and the email approaching the person needed to grant access and acquire 'informed consent' were important. Informally, more dynamic conceptions of consent are likely to involve discussing ideas and first impressions with parliamentary actors to (1) develop ideas and (2) ensure that the participants do not forget why you are there. In some ethnographic research of parties, all elements of transparency have not been followed, such as revealing party identification when reporting the findings (Bellè, 2016). With regard to informed consent, parliamentary researchers need to be pragmatic. MEPs were busy, consequently securing informed consent at the outset of a busy shadowing day was sometimes difficult, if we were attending a breakfast meeting, or being taken to see them in committee. Our strategy was to send all the project details well in advance and try to be very clear with the assistants, so in theory, at least, the MEP and their staff can be legitimately assumed to have read all documents about the project. In practice, we recognise that this is a grey area.

Remaining consistent with the principle that parliaments are publicly elected places and should be accountable, we were acutely aware that some participants may be in a position of vulnerability, especially staff. The pragmatic realities of informed consent, as well as the normative imperatives of being a critical researcher around social justice agendas matter; together they combine to impart a professional responsibility to the next cohort of researchers. We ensured the principles of no harm and anonymity by having a trusted colleague read the work and check that no one is identifiable or compromised.

Once inside the parliament, more bottom-up research access can be found through parliamentary researchers, Trade Union members and staff in the parliamentary administration. Immersion when inside the parliament can, to some extent, reject or at least ameliorate the affects of established gatekeepers. They might also value your research insights to be fed back to them. However, it should be borne in mind that staff might lose their influence due to staffing changes and rotations of responsibility.

ETHNOGRAPHIC PRACTICES

The choice of each research practice within Parliament may vary by research stage and by priorities. In terms of the degree of control over fieldwork, timing can be considered important with regard to the types of practices that are engaged in at each stage. An observation schedule is a loose itinerary of activities a researcher may wish to follow in a parliamentary ethnography, using the aforementioned parliamentary calendar. Planning can sometimes be accomplished. Nadia Brown (2014), for example, conducted a 'focused ethnography' of the Maryland legislature which is akin to Chappell et al.'s 'rapid ethnography' (2017). In a different example, Niemi's (2010: 75) study of the parliamentary administration in the Finnish Parliament, *Eduskunta*, was heavily guided by her exit from the field, which involved much data generation. In terms of the ability to plan in the European Parliament, timing and access in the electoral cycle and also unpredictable situations, in this case, Brexit deadlines and Covid, affected the planning of our ethnography.

We used three ethnographic research practices: shadowing, meeting ethnography and hanging out. First, shadowing is the practice of accompanying actors throughout their daily work lives, and was useful at the beginning of the research stage (Bussell, 2020: 471), to provide a generalised overview of the kinds of activities that MEPs participated in vis-à-vis their group. In general, shadowing helps guide a researcher in a field at the beginning. Emma Crewe uses an alternative term to shadowing and talks about 'following closely' her local MP. She describes one of the challenges she faced by saying that she 'had the perpetual feeling that I was in the wrong place at the wrong time' (2015: 5). We shadowed nine MEPs from five different political groups over a period of half a day to three days. We followed throughout their day and took notes on how they related to their political group. This also gave us important access to political group meetings.

Secondly, meetings are ubiquitous in the European Parliament, and meeting ethnography is developing conceptually as an analytically distinct practice that explores what meetings do (Brown et al., 2017; Sandler & Thedvall, 2017). The type of meetings attended may depend on the type of parliament and the form of activities. For the purpose of our research project, the political group meetings, working group meetings and national party delegation meetings were of interest. However, with the Covid-19 pandemic other meetings became important too, such as

President Sassoli's Press Conference on European Parliament's Covid-19 restrictions. We were able to observe and record in field notes how the group's 'top brass' were present for the Press Conference. We also recorded how attendees were filming the meeting, and how people were walking into the room later than the scheduled time, almost as if they knew the real routines and rhythms of the meeting.

Although some meetings were open in the parliament, in order to access others, we often asked an MEP's office if we could accompany them. To prepare, we asked in advance what the substantive content and political context of the meeting was like, and either the MEP or the assistant would sometimes provide a briefing. A chair, for example, allowed us into a pre-trilogue meeting. Prioritisation is equally important. Political groups hold their meetings in the same week, often at the same time, therefore researchers must prioritise and ask themselves, what is more important, group representation, or how a particular group, National Party Delegation or actor are going to behave if they come under fire? Such deliberations are not always easy.

Thirdly, in elite settings, the ethnographic practice of hanging out offers an alternative possibility for immersion. This is a more diffused and dialogic practice than meeting ethnography. Hanging out requires three facets: 'a period of continuous residence amid members of a field, engage[ment] in informal, ludic and sociable interactions sited outside or at the side-lines of members' professional habitats and participa[tion] in activities where striking and sustaining rapport is as important as the goals of the research' (Nair, 2021: 10). Densely clustered institutional spaces, such as the European Quarter, provide several immersive opportunities (Lewicki, 2017; Nair, 2021: 23). Being present also allows the researcher to recruit non-traditional participants. Hanging out, however, also creates demands—dealing with a posture of openness, transparency and reciprocity means the obligation to go to meetings or events that one is invited to. In terms of the research data that is achieved, hanging out provides better access to dissenting voices. For example, we observed dissenting voices from the civil society participants in the European Parliament's events on anti-racism (Kantola et al., 2023).

Finally, it is worth noting that other practices, such as interviews, can be conducted during the ethnographic fieldwork in high intensity. Nadia Brown, for example, conducted 49 interviews over a period of just nine days (2014: 185). This may reflect on the type of fieldwork relationship, trust and time with interlocutors that has been established. Similarly,

Emma Crewe compared UK MPs to UK Lords. She suggested 'peers are perfect informants: leisurely, candid and reflective. MPs are the opposite in every possible way' (Crewe, 2015: 5).

Conclusion

This chapter has discussed different aspects of gathering data through research interviews and parliamentary ethnography. Both the amount of preparatory work and the need to be creative, persistent and flexible were evident in our deliberations. The preparatory work included passing an ethical review, preparing forms, making decisions about whom to interview, considering different strategies to approach the interviewees, and doing background research about their political careers and work interests, all of which are undertaken prior to the interview or the ethnographic practice of shadowing. This required a constant willingness to evaluate the chosen strategies, interview questions and the ability to be reflexive when some choices were not bringing the desired outcomes. This chapter has strongly demonstrated the time-consuming and labour-intensive character of data gathering. Data analysis, which we turn in the next chapter, is no different in that sense.

References

Beckmann, M. N., & Hall, R. L. (2013). Elite interviewing in Washington, DC. In L. Mosley (Ed.), *Interview research in political science* (pp. 196–208). Cornell University Press.

Bellè, E. (2016). Knowing as being, knowing is being: Doing a political ethnography of an Italian right-wing party. *Anthropologie & Développement, 44*, 79–100.

Berthet, V., & Kantola, J. (2021). Gender, violence and political institutions: Struggles over sexual harassment in the European Parliament. *Social Politics, 28*(1), 143–167.

Bond, T. (2012). Ethical imperialism or ethical mindfulness? Rethinking ethical review for social sciences. *Research Ethics, 8*(2), 97–112.

Brinkmann, S. (2020). Unstructured and semi-structured interviewing. In P. Leavy (Eds.), *The Oxford handbook of qualitative research* (pp. 426–456, 2nd ed.). Oxford University Press.

Brown, N. E. (2014). *Sisters in the statehouse: Black women and legislative decision making*. Oxford University Press.

Brown, N. (2018). Negotiating the insider/outsider status: Black feminist ethnography and legislative studies. *Journal of Feminist Scholarship, 3*(3), 19–34.

Brown, H., Reed, A., & Yarrow, T. (2017). Introduction: Towards an ethnography of meeting. *Journal of the Royal Anthropological Institute, 23*(1), 10–26.

Busby, A. (2013). Normal Parliament': Exploring the organisation of everyday political life in an MEP's office. *Journal of Contemporary European Research, 9*(1), 94–115.

Bussell, J. (2020). Shadowing as a tool for studying political elites. *Political Analysis, 28*(4), 469–486.

Chappell, L. (2020). Doing elite interviews in feminist research: Confessions of a born-again observationist. In P. Wadds, N. Apoifis, S. Schmeidl, & K. Spurway (Eds.), *Navigating fieldwork in the social sciences: Stories of danger, risk and reward* (pp. 129–145). Palgrave Macmillan.

Chappell, L., Galea, N., & Waylen, G. (2017). Excavating informal institutional enforcement through 'rapid' ethnography: Lessons from the Australian construction industry. In G. Waylen (Ed.), *Gender and informal institutions* (pp. 67–89). Rowman & Littlefield.

Cowley, P. (2021). Interviewing MPs. https://ssrn.com/abstract=3764202

Crewe, E. (2015). *Commons and Lords: A short anthropology of Parliament*. Haus Publishing

Crewe, E. (2021). *The anthropology of parliaments: Entanglements in democratic politics*. Routledge.

Elomäki, A., & Ahrens, P. (2022). Contested gender mainstreaming in the European Parliament: Political groups and committees as gatekeepers. *European Journal of Politics and Gender, 5*(3), 322–340.

Evans, E., & Reher, S. (2022). Disability and political representation: Analysing the obstacles to elected office in the UK. *International Political Science Review, 43*(5), 697–712.

Firat, B. (2019). *Diplomacy and lobbying during Turkey's Europeanisation: The private life of politics*. Manchester University Press.

Fouché, C. B., & Chubb, L. A. (2017). Action researchers encountering ethical review: A literature synthesis on challenges and strategies. *Educational Action Research, 25*(1), 23–34.

Geddes, M., & Rhodes, R. A. W. (2018). Towards an interpretive parliamentary studies. In J. Brichzin, D. Krichewsky, L. Ringel, & J. Schank (Eds.), *Soziologie der Parlamente* (pp. 87–107). Springer.

Goplerud, M. (2021). Methods for analyzing parliamentary debates. In H. Back, M. Debus, & J. M. Fernandes (Eds.), *The politics of legislative debates*. Oxford University Press.

Holmes, G., Wright, K. A., Basu, S., Hurley, M., Martin de Almagro, M., Guerrina, R., & Cheng, C. (2019). Feminist experiences of 'studying up': Encounters with international institutions. *Millennium, 47*(2), 210–230.

Kantola, J., Elomäki, A., Gaweda, B., Miller, C., Ahrens, P., & Berthet, V. (2023). "It's like shouting to a brick wall": Normative whiteness and racism in the European Parliament. *American Political Science Review, 117*(1), 184–199.

Kantola, J., & Miller, C. (2022). Eternal friends or jubilant Brexiteers? The impact of Brexit on UK MEPs' parliamentary work in the European Parliament. *Journal of Common Market Studies.* Advance online publication. https:/ /doi.org/10.1111/jcms.13424

Laube, S. (2021). Material practices of ethnographic presence. *Journal of Contemporary Ethnography, 50*(1), 57–76.

Lewicki, P. (2017). *EU-space and the Euroclass: Modernity, nationality and lifestyle among Eurocrats in Brussels.* Transcript-Verlag Bielefeld.

Lilleker, D. G. (2003). Interviewing the political elite: Navigating a potential minefield. *Politics, 23*(3), 207–214.

Miller, C. (2021). Parliamentary ethnography and feminist institutionalism: Gendering institutions—But how? *European Journal of Politics and Gender, 4*(3), 361–380.

Miller, C. (2022). 'Ethno, ethno, what?': Using ethnography to explore the European Parliament's political groups in Turbulent Times. In P. Ahrens, A. Elomäki, & J. Kantola (Eds.), *European Parliament's political groups in Turbulent Times* (pp. 245–266). Palgrave Macmillan.

Molina, J. L., & Borgatti, S. P. (2021). Moral bureaucracies and social network research. *Social Networks, 67,* 13–19.

Muasya, J. N., & Gatumu, J. (2013). Ethical issues in researching discourses of sexual harassment in higher education: Experiences from the University of Nairobi, Kenya. *International Journal of Education and Research, 10*(1), 179–188.

Nair, D. (2021). Hanging 'out' while studying 'up': Doing ethnographic fieldwork in international relations. *International Studies Review, 23*(4), 1300–1327.

Niemi, H. (2010). *Managing in the "golden cage" an ethnographic study of work, management and gender in parliamentary administration* [Doctoral thesis]. Hanken School of Economics. https://helda.helsinki.fi/handle/10227/724

Reyes, V. (2018). Three models of transparency in ethnographic research: Naming places, naming people, and sharing data. *Ethnography, 19*(2), 204–226.

Ringe, N. (2022) *The language(s) of politics: Multilingual policy-making in the European Union.* University of Michigan Press.

Sandler, J., & Thedvall, R. (2017). *Meeting ethnography: Meetings as key technologies of contemporary governance, development, and resistance*. Routledge.

Sarikakis, K. (2003). A feminist in Brussels (and Glasgow, Berlin, Düsseldorf...) self-configuration in research into European Union Politics. *European Journal of Women's Studies, 10*(4), 423–441.

Soss, J. (2006). Talking our way to meaningful explanations: A practice-centered view of interviewing for interpretive research. In D. Yanow & P. Schwartz-Shea (Eds.), *Interpretation and method: Empirical research method and the interpretive turn* (pp. 127–149). M.E. Sharpe.

Verge, T. (2022). Evoking equality: The gender-sensitivity of parliaments through their symbolic function. *Political Studies, 70*(4), 1048–1067.

Wassenaar, D. R., & Mamotte, N. (2012). Ethical issues and ethics reviews in social science research. In A. Ferrero, Y. Korkut, M. M. Leach, G. Lindsay, & M. J. Stevens (Eds.), *The Oxford handbook of international psychological ethics* (pp. 268–282). Oxford University Press.

Weiss, R. S. (1994). *Learning from strangers: The art and method of qualitative interview studies*. Free Press.

CHAPTER 5

Coding the Data

Abstract Next to gathering qualitative data, coding of data lies at the core of qualitative research. The chapter is the first of two that dig into the specificities of data analysis. Coding is one way of organising dense data and making sense of it, for instance by identifying patterns. Whilst there exist various approaches to coding, this chapter presents a set of strategies to code dense interview, ethnographic and document data. Additionally, we present the technicalities of coding data collaboratively, as part of teamwork. Importantly, Chapter 5 yields important tips and concrete examples regarding the use of software tools for qualitative analysis, such as Atlas.ti and the intricacies of using it as a team. Specifically, the chapter discusses the initial stages of developing code lists in inductive and deductive ways, the technicalities pertaining to actually coding the text of the data with Atlas.ti, and presents an overview of the advantages of some tools, such as creating code families, to make sense of the data. Throughout the chapter, we discuss the collaborative nature of our coding work by reviewing the pros and cons and by examining issues pertaining to intercoder reliability.

Keywords Data analysis · Coding practices · ATLAS.ti · Teamwork · Benefits · Challenges

V. Berthet et al., *Guide to Qualitative Research in Parliaments*,
https://doi.org/10.1007/978-3-031-39808-7_5

INTRODUCTION

Coding organises dense data into manageable amounts and helps to make sense of it by revealing trends and patterns. Whilst Chapters 3 and 4 introduced the data and explained how it was gathered, the next two chapters are attentive to how we moved towards data analysis. Here we are concerned with the processes and strategies for coding qualitative data, whilst amongst other things, Chapter 6 looks more closely at rendering it more accessible to interpretation.

There are various ways to code qualitative research (Saldaña, 2021), but most coding processes typically trigger the emergence of dominant themes which can then be analysed (Coffey & Atkinson, 1996; Strauss, 1987). Whilst some see coding as a way to merely organise the data (Coffey & Atkinson, 1996), we see the organisation of the data as more than a preliminary stage prior to analysis (Weston et al., 2001); for us, coding and interpretation are necessarily intertwined (Corbin & Strauss, 2008; Tesch, 1990). Coding is an important element because it helps to make sense of the data in relation to one's research questions and objectives (Elliott, 2018) and sets rigorous foundations for its interpretation.

In practical terms, the coding process can be thought of as circulating between reading, coding and thinking about the raw material in terms of overarching concepts and categories, whilst also comparing and contrasting the coded material. This corresponds to adopting a flexible and iterative approach to coding, in the sense that it is possible to revise the initial code list and to code the data multiple times in a back-and-forth process that allows for recalibration and refinement, and the investigation of new research questions that emerge from the data (Yin, 2011). In practice, this means being open to the kind of patterns and 'meta-narratives' that can arise in the data, and concomitantly being willing to go back to 'square one' in terms of research assumptions and expectations.

This approach can be especially successful when new research themes, questions and eventually findings emerge through immersing oneself in, coding, discussing and interpreting data as an ongoing interaction rather than as separate stages. From our own experience, prominent illustrations of what such a strategy can bring include important findings that went beyond the main themes of our research project—'gender equality'—and extended to findings on racism (Kantola et al., 2023), Brexit (Kantola & Miller, 2023), the impact of the Covid-19 pandemic (Elomäki & Kantola,

2022) and on the role and powers of national party delegations in the European Parliament (Elomäki et al., 2023). These unforeseen insights were revealed by a flexible coding scheme in which we could collaboratively discuss missing themes in the initial code list, and develop additional codes as we were coding the data (Deterding & Waters, 2021). We applied systematic and transparent principles by keeping track of our discussions and decision-making processes in a research diary (see Box 5.1). In doing so, we respond to the lack of transparency regarding decision-making in collaborative research processes (Reyes et al., 2021), which we seek to make visible to other researchers here. For practical purposes, this meant that we all needed to be fully acquainted with the material, even if we were not the ones who conducted particular interviews.

Box 5.1 Examples of Team Research Diary Entries

- 'Coded my first two ethnographic fieldnotes. Feels quite different from interviews due to the structure. A lot more on affects and embodiment, very nice!' (EUGenDem research diary 19 Feb 2021)
- 'Was strange to code after such a long time! First I needed to re-read the code definitions to pick the right ones. And then it was a written one which has such a different flow... Was funny though that there were quite some affects in the responses, also regarding the researcher role!' (EUGenDem research diary 17 Nov 2020)
- 'A little difficult to follow—Interviewee sometimes talking about other things, such as her phone battery dying.' (EUGenDem research diary 17 March 2020)
- 'Surprising almost how little the interviewees talk about Covid, it is often present implicitly, in the goodbyes (stay safe, these strange times), or in references to having to postpone stuff or change plans'. (EUGenDem research diary 22 Feb 2021)
- 'I remember I had a feeling in the interview that the guy really didn't feel like talking to me and that everything I asked was somehow obvious to him. Reading the transcription through,

> it's not too tragic (even though rather short)'. (EUGenDem
> research diary 9 Nov 2020)

Due to the research design of our project, interviews and ethnography notes were compiled together in ATLAS.ti and coded collaboratively, whereas document data were selected and coded separately for the purpose of research articles according to their own research design and questions. Therefore, we begin by discussing the process of developing a collaborative coding strategy using ATLAS.ti, before discussing the challenges this posed for a large team of researchers, and presenting how documents were finally coded.

ATLAS.ti

ATLAS.ti was used to code and analyse our data. There are several scientific software packages for coding qualitative data but we opted for ATLAS.ti, not least because we had the expertise for this software within our team, and it was available freely (to us) through our institutions. The greatest volume of data we collected came in the form of interview data—the type of data for which ATLAS.ti is best suited. ATLAS.ti is best thought of as the vessel that houses the data, and along with researchers, facilitates a less complicated navigation through the coding process. In this sense, it stores and exchanges anonymised data; shares the workload of handling and coding dense data; keeps track of errors and inconsistencies amongst coders; and significantly highlights new ideas for codes. By using it collaboratively and extensively, that is by making full use of its functionality, helped respect the principles of transparency that are so important to the integrity of qualitative research (Reyes et al., 2021). The package offers export functions that enable the team to save and export entire 'projects'—including raw data, code-books, coding links and research diaries (memos). The latter is described by some as 'the substantive heart of qualitative data analysis' (Reyes et al., 2021, 6) as they keep track of researchers' reflections during the coding process, and help to make the decision-making process more transparent.

Whilst ATLAS.ti is self-explanatory and intuitive, some preparation from all the researchers is recommended, in particular if the team intends to code the data as it is gathered. Such preparation includes reading selected academic texts on software-based data coding (Ahrens, 2018; Friese, 2012; Paulus & Lester, 2016), familiarisation with the ATLAS.ti handbook and watching tutorial videos.[1] The fact that we had in our team a member who was already familiar and experienced with the use of such software was beneficial, as she could explain and teach ATLAS.ti to the rest of us. However this is by no means a precondition and ATLAS.ti does provide detailed instructions.

DEVELOPING A COLLABORATIVE CODING STRATEGY FOR INTERVIEWS AND ETHNOGRAPHIC DATA

Along with familiarity with ATLAS.ti, it was essential to develop a coding strategy. Both the design of the research project and the nature of the data gathered will influence the coding strategy. In our case, the coding strategy accommodated two levels of complexity: first, our data consisted of two different types of very dense data in the form of interview transcripts and ethnographic notes, and secondly, this had to be coded collaboratively. Our coding strategy combined the interviews and ethnographic data so they were treated as analogous and subjected to the same coding framework. This was our preference, although we acknowledge that scholars have debated this at great length, differing over how, and if at all, ethnographic data should be shared with other researchers (Contreras, 2019; Guenther, 2009; Jerolmack & Murphy, 2019; Reyes, 2018).

After gathering the first set of data, the team leapt straight into testing ATLAS.ti with everyone selecting one interview to code, applying any labels that emerged when reading. This process of inductive coding helped us to draft a list of initial codes (Chandra & Shang, 2019; Corbin & Strauss, 2008). Whilst much qualitative research adopts a deductive top-down approach by defining concepts first and coding second, we combined top-down and bottom-up approaches oriented towards grounded theory (Corbin & Strauss 2008; Creswell, 2013). A bottom-up approach means developing concepts and their dimensions inductively whilst coding. However, we contend it is not possible to analyse data without having pre-existing theoretical foundations in mind, as we are inevitably cognitive of (and arguably influenced by) them by

---

[1] See for instance https://atlasti.com/video-tutorials.

virtue of our knowledge of previous research. Thus, our initial list of inductive codes was completed by codes that were derived from the previous knowledge we gathered via reading groups and discussions of the literature as mentioned in Chapter 2.

The pilot study—or the first phase of data gathering (see Chapter 3)—offered a premium opportunity to develop and test a functioning collaborative coding process. Several focused team meetings served as the loci to collectively discuss, agree and develop a collaborative coding strategy. In these meetings, we agreed on broad definitions for each code and determined inclusive as well as exclusive criteria to explicitly clarify the situations in which each code would apply, using examples from our 'trial coding interviews'. This helped to ensure that the meaning of codes was understood by all, even those coders who joined the team later to promote intercoder reliability. Such meetings were crucial in taking important decisions that would enable us to code the data systematically, even though the way we split the workload meant that not everyone read nor coded all the data. For example, this included agreements on coding large chunks of text, and on the inclusion of interview questions so that each quotation would be in context and remain intelligible to those who did not code it.

Based on this first practical exercise, we compared codes and identified similarities, but also revealed several differences in the way we used codes. Here again the research diary and notes proved invaluable in keeping track of our observations, and often our doubts, as we often left questions to each other in the memos. The team member that chaired our meetings collected questions from all the diary notes and we addressed them together. The exercise was designed to improve intercoder reliability by discussing in detail our different understandings. We did not calculate intercoder reliability scores, but rather followed a more inclusive and collaborative approach for developing a code list, by defining the codes and determining how to use them. In other words, we refined and debated our choices collaboratively, so that understanding was consistent as it could be across all team members (Reyes et al., 2021). We explored recurring contradictions and solved them as part of subsequent brainstorming sessions, in which we added further codes inductively and deductively after the first rounds of coding.

The first code list was further refined and extended in comprehensive team meetings where two practical activities were undertaken to inspire code development. First, team members coded five interviews from their own ATLAS.ti project and were encouraged to develop new codes; this helped everyone to learn the technicalities of coding and to flag difficulties in doing so. Secondly, to counter the risk of early software-coding routines leading to narrow coding practice by using only certain codes, or using keyword searches instead of reading carefully, each team member hand-coded several interviews. Hand-coding is a technique that whilst considerably slowing down the coding process—it consists of flipping through printed material instead of scrolling on a screen—it tends to produce new codes.

We debated code names and definitions and jointly decided to ensure everyone used them correctly and systematically. This was one of the most important steps in the team coding process and re-occurred as a relevant practice throughout the coding stages. Clear definitions increase inter-coder reliability, ensure consistency in coding, train potential incoming members and make important interview segments visible to others. They must also specify what to include or exclude and when to use or not use the code. For instance, the code 'Sexism' was defined as instances where the interviewees 'describe sexism, sexist experiences, language; practices discriminating directly', whereas the code 'Gendered practices' was defined as 'all instances where genders are treated differently; speaking time, divisions of posts, vertical stuff; *not sexism*'. Furthermore, three additional subcodes completed the code 'Gendered practices': 'Gendered practices_discrimination', 'Gendered practices_division of labour' and 'Gendered practices_hierarchies'. Each of these had a specific definition that differentiated them. For example, we defined 'Gendered practices_discrimination' as instances where, 'the word is used, also including mentions of bias, indirect discrimination etc.'; 'Gendered practices_division of labour' as highlighting the 'separation of women's and men's policy areas' in interviews; and 'Gendered practices_hierarchies' as all instances where the interviewees mentioned 'women having difficulties getting reports, leadership positions etc. vertical segregation'.

Without clear definitions, such a collaborative, supportive and inclusive team coding process would not have been possible and would have obscured key elements of the data. Trusting each other to signpost important and relevant topics within the dense data was key to the success of the research project and considerably speeded up the process. Simply put, the first stage of coding allowed us to categorise the raw data under important and jointly developed topics, which then helped individual researchers to investigate them further. Without this, the screening and coding of all the dense data for each individual study would have been far too time-consuming and overwhelming.

In our view, codes and definitions should not be 'set in stone' because the coding process requires their constant adjustment and extension. We followed this practice whilst the project was in full flow, with the consequence that we re-coded interviews depending on what revisions were implied. For example, if a code was split into two, we also re-coded the respective code segments and ensured that the new codes were applied to other quotations where appropriate. Likewise, when we merged codes, we re-coded the relevant data.

Our iterative approach to coding meant that we could complement our initial list of codes with new codes that emerged at later stages of the research process. We complemented and informed our list of codes deductively with ideas from literature, documentary research, and on the basis of pre-selected keywords relevant to the main objectives of the project. These included, for instance, 'democratic practices', 'political groups', 'economy', 'gender-based violence', 'affects' or 'social policy'. Whilst inductively, we supplemented the list of codes with emerging themes, such as 'political group meetings', 'resistance to gender equality' or 'sexual harassment'. In total, the first brainstorming sessions resulted in a list of 99 codes, including 55 main codes and 44 subcodes; where subcodes were the code families for main codes.

Codes that were added during the process of reading and re-coding of the material, were the starting point of many of our published findings; they were not initially planned, but made possible because we diligently travelled back-and-forth between coding and new analysis of the data. For instance, we extracted unexpected insights from our data on the power dynamics of national party delegations in the European Parliament, because we added the code 'National party delegations' (Elomäki et al., 2023), on normative whiteness and racism consequent upon the added code 'intersectionality_race' (Kantola et al., 2023) and the role of gendered religious claims after the addition of the code 'religion' (Ahrens et al., 2022).

MANAGING THE TECHNICALITIES
OF COLLABORATIVE CODING

In addition to the intellectual work of designing a code strategy that was applicable to all researchers, team coding required finding solutions for technical and organisational issues intrinsic to the project (see Box 5.4). The shifting geographical locations of team members had an additional impact on the process, and not least, the Covid-19 pandemic had a profound impact on planned in-person meetings which became impossible for an extended period.

The team being split between places became problematic when we worked on a joint ATLAS.ti 'project'—as recommended by ATLAS.ti. We initially planned to place the so-called 'copy bundle'—that is the exported ATLAS.ti 'project', including all coded and raw data, list of codes, information on codes and memos—in our joint drive at Tampere University. However, this turned out to be impossible as running ATLAS.ti via VPN on personal laptops often failed. Instead, for the pilot study, we decided to follow the second option recommended by ATLAS.ti, whereby every team member sets up their own ATLAS.ti 'project' with the interviews assigned to them, and then one team member would merge all the projects. Nevertheless, with the high number of team members coding simultaneously this proved to be impractical. Whilst the coded interviews were rather unproblematic when compiled, shared or revised, memos were not easily merged and had to be put together manually—a step which would have been far too time-consuming.

As a result, we agreed on a different sharing process for the main study. One team member was 'in charge' of the copy bundle, of which they supervised, managed and controlled the whole coding process. That person assigned interviews to each team member who was then responsible for coding. This meant that each team member coded certain interviews, including the ones not available in English but in their mother tongue. We established a rotation system with one coder coding at a time in the same ATLAS.ti 'project', before exporting it as a copy bundle and sending it via university email to the next coder in line. The rotation system respected a clear order of names (e.g., coder A before coder B; and coder E after coder D) with each coder knowing who coded before them and who would receive the copy bundle after them.

Similarly, the person in charge assigned interviews on a rolling basis, typically two interviews per round, and coders knew approximately which day of the week the copy bundle would come to them. They could thus reserve time for their allocated day to code the two interviews and send it to the next coder in time. We built in a degree of flexibility to allow for the possibility that days might need to be switched with another coder, but this needed to be clear to the whole team so that the entire process kept rolling smoothly, and did not affect the allocation of interviews which remained the same.

To ensure that nothing got lost in the process of exchanging copy bundles, we created one single email thread for sending them and all the information related to coding. Whenever someone finished their coding, they would send the new copy bundle in this thread along with important features of the interviews that needed to be flagged up. Every Thursday, the copy bundle would return to the team member in charge, who would add new interview data as they came back from transcription and allocate them to coders for the upcoming coding weeks. This 'rolling coding' strategy meant that with six coders, each coder had a coding-free day every other week due to the maximum of four coding days per week. During the project, we sometimes had to code with fewer people due to long fieldwork periods, illness, or care responsibilities during lockdowns.

As well as coding, the team member in charge was responsible for all other technical issues. Each Friday, they checked the latest copy bundle, saved it and resolved errors, a task made easier by the research diary—or 'memo'—as we kept all the entries made by the coders in one place. In fact, each coder had to report on the research diary after each coding session. The research diary turned out to be a central element to our coding strategy, as it made the collective coding process transparent to other coders, kept track of ideas or thoughts whilst coding, highlighted errors or inconsistencies, and significantly, stressed any doubts that needed to be discussed in upcoming meetings. All the minutes from coding meetings were also stored as a memo directly on the ATLAS.ti 'project', as a means of increasing access and transparency during coding. In fact, these very lines are written on the basis of the notes we kept in the research diary throughout the coding process. Each coder recorded aspects like new ideas for codes, problems with coding or specific interviews, questions to discuss in meetings and also comments on funny quotes, oddities or levity in the interviews (see Boxes 5.2 and 5.3). After the basic checkup, the person in charge uploaded new anonymised transcripts, allocated them to coders, and documented everything in the research diary.

Box 5.2 Examples from Our Research Diary of Exchange of Thoughts Whilst Coding

- 'I coded the interview 'Renew MEP M 081,119 Brexit'. I understand that it was particularly meant for the Brexit paper, but was still a bit surprised that other main questions from our interview list were not addressed. Would have been interesting to gather more information on gender aspects, too.' (EUGenDem research diary 27 Jan 2020)
- 'What struck me most when comparing these two interviews is the stark contrast of how the two describe their start and how gendered it is: the female says it is hard to get into positions because there are of course many returning MEPs who can choose first and she'll have to wait; the male says he was surprised how easy it was to get the position he wants and how many requests he got.' (EUGenDem research diary 22 Apr 2020)
- 'I feel that in Zoom meetings it is hard to build rapport and it is easier for participants to say: 'I've got to be somewhere in half an hour' because you have spent less effort going to meet them in person in the parliament.' (EUGenDem research diary 13 Nov 2020)
- 'Since coding the notes, I would really see the need for the 'power relations' code—political influence just doesn't cover what is in the notes.' (EUGenDem research diary 25 Feb 2021)
- 'I like that when coding ethnographic notes I get to use the codes that I felt I was often underusing when coding the interviews: 'embodiment', 'EP spaces', 'researcher role', etc.' (EUGenDem research diary 13 Apr 2021)
- 'A usual issue came up with codes, which is whether to include a code when it is referred to in the negative e.g. the EP as a unique parliament. I coded the section as this, even though the respondent says that it isn't a unique parliament.' (EUGenDem research diary 28 Jan 2020)

> **Box 5.3 Moments of Levity in Our Interviews that We Highlighted to Each Other in the Research Diary**
>
> - 'I would also say that men are often the ones who have been in parliament for a longer time. So, those [persons/men] who have divided things here already for three or four terms; the others are still searching for the toilets, and while they still don't know where the toilets are in the house, the men have the jobs already divided' (Female S&D MEP March 2020)
> - During an interview in the midst of the Covid-19 restrictions: 'Thank you. I think I'm a little... I haven't been speaking to anyone this week and so maybe that's why I don't find the words.' (Female Left assistant March 2020)
> - 'X comes back to the office. X says 'I must go, I am late for my life' and their assistant notes that this is a pithy saying and outlook.' (Ethnographic field note shadowing a female EPP MEP November 2018)
> - 'R: Talking about, you had some extraordinary word in there I had never heard of before, ethno-something-or...
>
>   I: Ethnography...
>   R: Never heard of it.' (Male ENF MEP February 2019)
>
> - 'We don't believe in the European Union, so we're just here because we want to destroy it.' (Male EFDD MEP January 2019)
> - 'They say politics is rock music for ugly people.' (Male ENF MEP February 2019)

We put each newly uploaded interview transcript into document groups, covering categories like the political group, female/male, MP/Staff/ and nationality. As will be explained below, this simplified both code outputs and the analysis. Then, if applicable, the team member in charge would create, revise or merge[2] codes as agreed in team coding meetings. When

---

[2] Merging codes means combining two or more previous codes into one new code, for instance, when previous codes were too detailed and resulted in very low numbers of coded material that could be equally well represented by one overarching code.

all these steps were completed, the new copy bundle was sent in the email thread with an overview of who was next in the rotation system (with dates), and the process would begin again. Finally, our person in charge collected questions, code proposals and any other business to be presented and discussed during the next coding meeting.

Once we finished coding most of the interview data, we moved on to the ethnographic data using the list of codes we had already developed. The ethnographic notes were an excellent way to contextualise interview data and elicit new perspectives. In the interest of simplicity and clarity, we used the existing list of codes rather than developing new ones, which was justified by the already extensive (and saturated) list of codes (in total 112 codes) we had already generated (see Box 5.5).

Overall, the strategy of collective 'rolling coding' ensured that the data was very quickly available after transcription for further analysis and interpretation. Furthermore, such a closely intertwined and intrinsically collective process kept all coders in the loop, encouraged constant cross-comparison between coders, and resulted in fruitful in-depth discussions of potential research questions that emerged from the data (see Box 5.4). The flexibility we built into a process that utilised so many coders, allowed us to be reflexive in response to people's changing circumstances and unforeseen complications. Nonetheless, our periodic coding meetings revealed only minimal dissimilarities in the ways in which coders understood some codes, which was a testament to the constant and transparent communication required amongst all coders. Given the differences in research foci, and the very high number of codes, coders did not always, systematically attend to all of the codes, which at times left parts of the data less visible. To address this issue, we organised additional rounds of coding where all coders rechecked their assigned interviews for occurrences of specific codes, and invested additional time on an ongoing basis to assess where the coding process stands and to engage in discussions.

Box 5.4 Core Points for Successful Collective Coding

- Develop the code list with code names and definitions collectively (mention situational inclusion and exclusion, if necessary).
- Allow for constant adjustment of codes, their definitions, adding new ones and for splitting/merging existing ones.
- Trust your choice of codes, whether they are deductively or inductively developed, and encourage using codes as often as possible.
- Ensure communication transparency has the highest priority: establish a research diary for the whole team to collect notes and ideas on the process for extending and adjusting codes; share all information related to coding in one email thread or drive folder.
- Appoint one person in charge: a team member, researcher, and coder that supervises and manages the collective coding process. This person's tasks need to include collecting remarks from the research diary and raising them for discussion in team coding meetings.
- Make a clear plan including responsibilities for everyone but allow for flexibility and be prepared for interruptions.
- Try to keep the coding and discussion process continuously rolling to make the most of memorising content and technicalities.

Organising and Sorting the Coded Interview and Ethnographic Data

Once the raw interview and ethnographic notes were coded, we applied two main sorting mechanisms to make sense of our coded data. We used 'code groups' and 'document groups'—functions defined by ATLAS.ti. 'Code groups' offered the opportunity to select specific topics, such as specific policy fields, parliamentary bodies, actors, relationships or affects, whereas 'document groups' categorised interviews along specific descriptive categories, such as male/female or MEPs/staff and per political groups or nationalities. This allowed us to work with coded data quickly for such descriptive groups, making our dense data more manageable and analyzable, by extracting quotations that intersect with one code and one political group (eg., 'sexual harassment' and 'EPP').

In total, our ATLAS.ti project included 112 different codes, made up of 69 main codes and 43 subcodes grouped into 16 code families, which helped bridge codes that complemented each other on similar themes (see Table 5.1 for examples). Other functions of ATLAS.ti, such as 'output tables' or 'reports of co-occurring codes' and 'reports of neighbouring codes' provided an easy way to extract data for analysis.

Box 5.5 Different Types of Codes

The codes comprised different kinds with the following constituting the main aspects:

- Codes relating to process and sequencing: when and how political groups were formed? how specific policy proposals moved through different stages? (e.g., 'political group formation', 'democratic practices', 'EP elections 2019'; 'political group internal policy formation', 'political influence');
- Codes related to policy fields (e.g., economic policy, gender-based violence and social policy);
- Codes on specific topics (e.g., 'leadership', 'civil society', 'opposition to gender equality', 'gender mainstreaming', 'reproductive rights', 'Covid-19' and 'Brexit');
- Codes for internal communication, either ethical aspects or reminders to ourselves for further steps, such as new names for interviews or requests for the confidentiality of single comments (e.g., 'researcher role', 'to follow-up', 'confidential text in interview');
- Codes on relationships between actors inside and outside the European Parliament (e.g. 'Europarties', 'political groups about other political groups', 'MEPs vis-a-vis political groups', 'negotiations and compromise between political groups' and 'interinstitutional relationships');

- Codes on certain bodies and functions (e.g., 'political groups identity', 'political groups organisation', 'National party delegations', 'EP administration', 'Secretary General', 'rapporteurs', 'coordinators');
- Codes on internal practices (e.g., 'political groups as workplace', 'political groups conflicts_internal', 'MEPs daily work');
- Other relevant codes (e.g., 'racism', 'Spitzenkandidatur', 'religion', 'sexism', 'feminism', 'populism', 'Euroscepticism').

By creating 'document groups', researchers were able to extract all data relevant to their research questions at once. For instance, if analysing the gendered aspects of leadership in political groups, researchers could quickly extract the relevant data by exporting quotes that intersect with the document groups 'Greens/EFA political group' and 'female MEPs', and with the code group 'leadership'. Working with such combinations extracts data in ways that make further analysis manageable by restricting the searched volume of data to the most relevant part. This was particularly helpful for codes that we applied often. The code 'National party delegations', for example, generated roughly 500 quotations or over 200 pages of coded data. Intersecting that code with other 'document groups' or 'code groups' helped simplify the process of data analysis. Thus, when combining the code 'National party delegations' with the document group of all political groups, we generated 42 pages of coded data—making the data analysis considerably more manageable.

ATLAS.ti includes various tools that help to organise, sort and make sense of the coded data in view of interpreting it. Some tools allowed for the tracking of connected codes, concepts and theoretical thoughts that emerged whilst coding. For instance, coders were able to link codes and quotations with relations such as 'contradicts', 'is associated with' or 'is part of'. ATLAS.ti easily allowed the application, merging, or splitting of codes, and writing and attaching memos to any part of the data deemed relevant. More advanced features included sorting the coded data into networks of codes, which helped to quickly visualise the co-occurrences of codes and the relations between quotations. As a result, and by playing with and visualising the coded data differently, researchers can become more familiar with its material and develop a 'professional vision' towards it (Goodwin, 1994, in Elliott, 2018).

Table 5.1 Examples of code families

Code family	Main code	Subcodes	Definition	Occurrences
Affects	Affects		Descriptions of emotions and affects, strong language and figures in the interviews, expressions of emotions in the interviews	349
		Affective atmospheres	More collective, more mood, e.g. in locale/e.g. group meeting 'tense' or 'business like'	211
		Expression of emotions	Cognitive, more isolated/interviewed expresses an emotion or uses emotional language	253
Committee	Committee		Including: all committees, interactions and division of competences between them, etc.	318
		ECON	Mentions of ECON	177
		EMPL	Mentions of EMPL	89
		FEMM	Mentions of FEMM	178
		LIBE	Mentions of LIBE	89

(continued)

Table 5.1 (continued)

Code family	Main code	Subcodes	Definition	Occurrences
Gender equality	Gender equality		How gender equality is referred to and used by the interviewee	292
		Policies	References to different gender quality policies, such as equal pay, reconciling work and family, violence, gender mainstreaming	162
		Practices	Practices to promote gender equality, quotas, harassment policies, women's networks, training, and groups. Not FEMM	75
		EP	European Parliament specific practices for promoting gender equality	73
		PG	Political groups specific practices for promoting gender equality	186
		Descriptive representation	Gender balance and mentions thereof	

Code family	Main code	Subcodes	Definition	Occurrences
PG organisation	PG organisation		Description of bodies, structures, functions, funding, budgets	223
		Group meeting	Mentions of Group meeting	219
		Press office	Activities of PG press office	74
		Statues	Mentions of Statues	40
Sexism	Sexism		They describe sexism, sexiest experiences, language; practices discriminating directly	74
		Good expertise	Stereotyped expertise (masculine/feminine)	45
		Sexiest language	Description of interviewees when sexiest language was used	20

In sum, most of ATLAS.ti's tools and functions help to zoom in on specific narratives, rhetoric and frames under one or more code(s), allowing a closer reading of our data in relation to our research questions.

CODING DOCUMENTS FOR RESEARCH ARTICLE

Whilst all the researchers coded our interview and ethnographic data, document data was coded separately for each individual research article. Nonetheless, this followed a similar pattern of organising dense data into manageable chunks, and preparing the text for interpretation. In this respect, we followed the approach to coding that envisaged an evolving, rather than fixed strategy, to be used throughout the project-related publications (Elliott, 2018). In that sense, the coding strategies developed for research articles largely depended on their research questions.

As Chapter 3 showed, we collected a wealth of internal documents from the EP including practice (e.g., rules of procedure and codes of conduct) and policy-related documents (e.g., reports, amendments, position papers and press releases). We gathered such documents on a case-by-case basis, dependent on the research design and research question germane to a specific research article. As a result, we coded documents according to frameworks developed by the researcher(s) in charge of the article: either single or group coding approaches (see Box 5.6). On occasion, this framework was used to code both the document data, and to re-code chunks of coded interview and ethnographic data. In these instances, the interview and ethnographic data were coded in a first stage of collective coding, as explained above, and then re-coded along with additional material such as documents with a coding strategy (i.e., a new code list, code definition, etc....) developed for the research article. For example, in one research article we focused on the policy-related issue of the ratification of the Istanbul Convention on violence against women and domestic violence by the EU. At the first stage of collective coding, the code 'Istanbul Convention' was applied to any mention of it in the interview and ethnographic data. At the second stage of coding for individual study, the research design and research question required the expansion of research material to include specific documents, such as transcripts of debates, and the re-coding of the pre-coded data under 'Istanbul Convention' in a separate ATLAS.ti 'project' with a new list of tailored codes (Berthet, 2022a). Both the document data and the pre-coded interview and ethnographic data were re-coded with the same code list developed at the second stage of coding to ensure a systematic process.

Coding documents is demanding. Written records of amendments and debates, for example, can be lengthy, consisting of large amounts of text that need to be closely analysed. By way of illustration, we analysed over 1090 amendments for the pay transparency draft directive and 750 for the work-life balance draft directive (Copeland et al., 2023). The more salient the topic, the greater the amount of amendments there were to analyse. For instance, the non-legislative draft report on sexual and reproductive health and rights in the EU, which included provisions on abortion rights, generated over 500 amendments at the committee level (Berthet, 2022b). Similarly, a plenary debate on a salient topic could include over 500 oral and written interventions. In this sense, coding document data was useful for reducing the data into 'manageable proportions' (Coffey & Atkinson, 1996, 28).

A recurrent form of document data was amendments made by MEPs and political groups to committee reports. Whilst these are important when analysing policy processes, because they allow for the identification of group positions that are taken, we adopted different approaches to coding amendments for different research articles. When a study was attentive to different discursive constructions, we selected and coded those amendments that were relevant to the discursive analysis of one specific issue (e.g., abortion rights). Equally, when a study was interested in identifying group positions and comparing them in a quantifiable way, we coded all amendments made to a specific report (e.g., how often groups weakened the proposals and which groups) (Copeland et al., 2023).

Box 5.6 Coding Document Data for Research Articles

We coded documents based on our interest in specific policy issues, for instance, abortion rights (Berthet, 2022b), economic policy (Elomäki, 2021), economic and social rights (Elomäki & Gaweda, 2022), austerity politics (Elomäki, forthcoming) and strategies of opposition to gender equality (Berthet, 2022a; Kantola &

Lombardo, 2021a, 2021b). We also coded documents to investigate the influence of groups on Commission Directive proposals (Copeland et al., 2023) and the power dynamics and modes of decision-making in groups (Elomäki et al., 2022). In these cases, coding had an analytical function; it helped with '(a) noticing relevant phenomena, (b) collecting examples of those phenomena, and (c) analysing those phenomena in order to find commonalities, differences, patterns, and structures' (Seidel & Kelle, 1995, 55–56).

Because we coded documents based on the research question(s) specifically developed for each research article (see Box 5.7), the coding lists were developed deductively and inductively according to the specific theoretical and epistemological approaches taken (Coffey & Atkinson, 1996, 32). In some cases, the development of codes took place in multiple steps, starting from the descriptive level and moving towards analytical typologies. This confirms that our coding was dynamic, and influenced by theory-driven interpretation(s), as well as analytical.

Box 5.7 Example of a Coding Strategy for a Research Article

In one research article on economic ideas about austerity and its alternatives in the European Parliament, (Elomäki, forthcoming), amendments and plenary interventions related to ten of the EP's own initiative reports on EU economic governance, were initially coded through a code list that involved four categories: (i) approach to austerity (opposing/supporting), (ii) rationales for supporting austerity, (iii) rationales for opposing austerity and (iv) alternatives to austerity. The categories ii–iv involved several options each, deducted from a combination of existing scholarship and matters that emerged from the data. In the analysis and writing process, the emphasis moved from rationales to paradigms. The final coding of the data consisted of classifying the amendments and plenary interventions into three main pro-austerity paradigms and three main paradigms providing alternatives.

Some of the ATLAS.Ti tools, for instance, the co-occurrence and query functions, eventually helped us identify patterns of meanings (Bazeley, 2009a). In this respect, during the adoption of a report, we were able to observe how some political groups in the European Parliament discussed public services more often as a cost or as an investment. Likewise, we could assess if and how they discussed gender equality via economic rationales or as a value in itself.

Although our analysis was always qualitative, some of us used the possibilities provided by ATLAS.ti to generate quantified comparisons (Bazeley, 2009b). Although quantifying was for us often a preliminary step, with our emphasis being discursive-interpretive analysis, journal reviewers often asked specifically for quantified data—which we were happy and able to provide. Our process meant that we could compare the distribution of amendments from political groups that either strengthened, weakened, or verified/clarified a specific draft directive, allowing us to see at a glance where political groups stood relative to each other, or how the patterns of strengthening and weakening differed by directive. Quantification was also useful to understand patterns of change over time in those cases where longitudinal analysis of recurring EP reports was conducted. Through the code/document function of ATLAS.ti, we could observe shifts in the positions adopted by EP as well as political groups—for instance, a shift from austerity to investment in at least some EPP MEPs discourse, or how the initial acceptance of austerity by some S&D MEPs in the early 2010s turned into an outright rejection (Elomäki, forthcoming).

Since our research objectives concentrated mostly on the lines of convergence and conflict between the groups, it was important to identify them correctly. Consequently, when documents covering amendments and debates were coded, for example, we paid particular attention to the political affiliation of the speakers. Ensuring the integrity of our identification often required extra work, which was particularly the case with amendments, as they were not always attributable to a particular group. It also became important to note the nationalities of MEPs since fault lines in groups and cross-group alliances tend to form on the basis of shared nationalities. Such codes are descriptive but necessary for later analysis (Elliott, 2018; see Box 5.5).

Similar to the challenges of coding interview data collectively, when problems relating to different interpretations of codes and content emerged during co-authorship, we strove for intercoder reliability via discussion and interaction during the coding process. This included several discussions about our coding framework and definitions, testing the coding framework before starting the actual coding work and comparing it. For example, co-authors exchanged parts of the coded data to see if others would have coded it differently, and any emergent differences were addressed and settled in our resolve to ensure transparency in coding-related decision-making.

Conclusion

Like any other aspect of the research process, data coding using analytical software provides benefits and challenges. As we have demonstrated, coding is one way of organising dense data and of making sense of it by identifying overarching patterns. Whilst various approaches to coding exist, this chapter was attentive to the strategies we implemented to code dense interview, ethnographic and document data collaboratively. We have provided important tips and concrete examples of using software tools for qualitative analysis, such as ATLAS.ti, and the intricacies of using it as a team. Specifically, we addressed the initial stages of developing code lists in inductive and deductive ways, the technicalities intrinsic to coding the text of the data with ATLAS.ti, and presented an overview of how we took advantage of some tools, such as creating code families, to make sense of the data. Our main focal point throughout the chapter was to highlight the collaborative nature of our coding work by reviewing the pros and cons, and by examining how issues of intercoder reliability were resolved. Our approach to data analysis was firmly rooted in collaborative work and provided the basis for all further interpretative analysis through individual or co-authored research articles, as well as collaboration with external scholars. Having a more nuanced understanding of the processes we followed, and the techniques we established throughout the coding process, provides a firm foundation to better understand our interpretation of the results, which the discussion of we turn to next.

References

Ahrens, P. (2018). Qualitative network analysis: A useful tool for investigating policy networks in transnational settings? *Methodological Innovations, 11*(1), 1–9.

Ahrens, P., Gaweda, B., & Kantola, J. (2022). Reframing the language of human rights? Political group contestations on women's and LGBTQI rights in European Parliament debates. *Journal of European Integration, 44*(6), 803–819.

Bazeley, P. (2009a). Analysing qualitative data: More than 'identifying themes.' *Malaysian Journal of Qualitative Research, 2*(2), 6–22.

Bazeley, P. (2009b). Integrating data analyses in mixed methods research. *Journal of Mixed Methods Research, 3*(3), 203–207.

Berthet, V. (2022a). Norm under fire: Support for and opposition to the European Union's ratification of the Istanbul Convention in the European Parliament. *International Feminist Journal of Politics, 24*(5), 675–698.

Berthet, V. (2022b). United in Crisis: Abortion Politics in the European Parliament and Political Groups' Disputes over EU Values. *Journal of Common Market Studies, 60*(6), 1797–1814.

Chandra, Y., & Shang, L. (2019). Inductive coding. In Y. Chandra & L. Shang (Eds.), *Qualitative research using R: A systematic approach* (pp. 91–106). Springer Singapore.

Coffey, A., & Atkinson, P. (1996). *Making sense of qualitative data: Complementary research strategies*. Sage Publications.

Corbin, J., & Strauss, A. L. (2008). *Basics of qualitative research : Techniques and procedures for developing grounded theory*. Sage.

Contreras, R. (2019). The broken ethnography: Lessons from an almost hero. *Qualitative Sociology, 42,* 161–179.

Copeland, P., Elomäki, A., & Gaweda, B. (2023). Filtering politicization towards a more social Europe? The European Parliament's role in EU legislation. Paper presented at the 29th International Conference of Europeanists, 27–29 June 2023, University of Reykjavik, Iceland.

Creswell, J. (2013). *Qualitative inquiry and research design*. Sage.

Deterding, N. M., & Waters, M. C. (2021). Flexible coding of in-depth interviews: A twenty-first-century approach. *Sociological Methods & Research, 50*(2), 708–739.

Elliott, V. (2018). Thinking about the coding process in qualitative data analysis. *The Qualitative Report, 23*(11), 2850–2861.

Elomäki, A. (2021). "It's a total no-no": The strategic silence about gender in the European Parliament's economic governance policies. *International Political Science Review*. https://doi.org/10.1177/019251212097832

Elomäki, A. (Forthcoming). Austerity and its alternatives in the European Parliament: From the Eurozone crisis to the Covid-19. *Comparative European Politics*.

Elomäki, A., & Gaweda, B. (2022). Looking for the 'Social' in the European Semester: The ambiguous 'Socialisation'of EU Economic Governance in the

European Parliament. *Journal of Contemporary European Research, 18*(1), 166–183.

Elomäki, A., Gaweda, B., & Berthet, V. (2022). Democratic Practices and Political Dynamics of Intra-Group Policy Formation in the European Parliament. In P. Ahrens, A. Elomäki, & J. Kantola (Eds.), *European Parliament's Political Groups in Turbulent Times* (pp. 73–96). Springer International Publishing.

Elomäki, A., & Kantola, J. (2022). Feminist governance in the European Parliament: The political struggle over the inclusion of gender in the EU's COVID-19 response. *Politics & Gender*, 1-22, https://doi.org/10.1017/S1743923X21000544

Elomäki, A., Kantola, J., Ahrens, P., Berthet, V., Gaweda, B., & Miller, C. (2023). The politics of national delegations in the European Parliament. Paper presented at the Center for European Studies (CES) Seminar on Researching the European Union, 1 February 2023. University of Helsinki, Finland.

Friese, S. (2012). *Qualitative Data Analysis with ATLAS.ti*. Sage.

Goodwin, C. (1994). Professional vision. *American Anthropologist, 96*(3), 606–633.

Guenther, K. M. (2009). The politics of names: Rethinking the methodological and ethical significance of naming people, organizations, and places. *Qualitative Research, 9*(4), 411–421.

Jerolmack, C., & Murphy, A. K. (2019). The ethical dilemmas and social scientific trade-offs of masking in ethnography. *Sociological Methods & Research, 48*(4), 801–827.

Kantola, J., Elomäki, A., Gaweda, B., Miller, C., Ahrens, P., & Berthet, V. (2023). "It's Like Shouting to a Brick Wall": Normative Whiteness and Racism in the European Parliament. *American Political Science Review, 117*(1), 184–199.

Kantola, J., & Miller, C. (2023). Eternal Friends or Jubilant Brexiteers? The Impact of Brexit on UK MEPs' Parliamentary Work in the European Parliament. *Journal of Common Market Studies, 61*, 712–729.

Kantola, J., & Lombardo, E. (2021a). Strategies of right populists in opposing gender equality in a polarized European Parliament. *International Political Science Review, 42*(5), 565–579.

Kantola, J., & Lombardo, E. (2021b). Challenges to democratic practices and discourses in the European Parliament: Feminist perspectives on the politics of political groups. *Social Politics, 28*(3), 579–602.

Paulus, T. M., & Lester, J. N. (2016). ATLAS.ti for conversation and discourse analysis studies. *International Journal of Social Research Methodology, 19*(4), 405–428.

Reyes, V., Bogumil, E., & Welch, L. E. (2021). The living codebook: Documenting the process of qualitative data analysis. *Sociological Methods & Research*. https://doi.org/10.1177/0049124120986185

Reyes, V. (2018). Three models of transparency in ethnographic research: Naming places, naming people, and sharing data. *Ethnography*, *19*(2), 204–226.

Saldaña, J. (2021). *The coding manual for qualitative researchers*. Sage Publications.

Seidel, J., & Kelle, U. (1995). Different functions of coding in the analysis of textual data. In U. Kelle (Ed.), *Computer-aided qualitative data analysis: Theory, methods and practice* (pp. 52–61). Sage.

Strauss, A. L. (1987). *Qualitative analysis for social scientists*. Cambridge University Press.

Tesch, R. (1990). *Qualitative research : analysis types and software tools*. Falmer Press.

Weston, C., Gandell, T., Beauchamp, J., McAlpine, L., Wiseman, C., & Beauchamp, C. (2001). Analyzing interview data: The development and evolution of a coding system. *Qualitative Sociology*, *24*, 381–400.

Yin, R. (2011). *Qualitative Research from Start to Finish*. The Guilford Press.

CHAPTER 6

Interpreting the Data

Abstract Once the data (or part of it) is coded it becomes possible
to move on to the next step, which is to interpret the data in view of
answering research questions. Interpreting the data is a crucial step in the
qualitative research process—it is core to qualitative data analysis. Hence,
the volume dedicates a whole chapter to it. This Chapter presents key
methodological steps and strategies to interpret the data for the purpose
of individual studies for peer-reviewed articles. It covers practical steps
such as exporting code reports from Atlas.ti and reviewing them in a
collaborative fashion. It also includes methodological steps, such as the
review of epistemological reflections pertaining to interpreting qualitative data. The chapter further digs into the specificities of interpreting
frames and discourses from coded qualitative data, but also interpreting
formal and informal practices from 'text' and, finally, extracting information about the parliamentary policy processes. The chapter provides
a guide to conducting qualitative analysis driven by research questions
that are inherently constructivist, interpretivist and/or post-structuralist.
In particular, we explore how qualitative data can be interpreted in a way
that sheds light on the power dynamics, genderedness and informality of
parliamentary work.

Keywords Interpretative strategies · Research question · Discourses ·
Policy tracing · Formal practices · Informal practices

© The Author(s) 2023   107
V. Berthet et al., *Guide to Qualitative Research in Parliaments*,
https://doi.org/10.1007/978-3-031-39808-7_6

Introduction

The previous chapter outlined the strategies and specific steps we took to code interview, ethnographic and documentary qualitative data collaboratively. This chapter explores the epistemological and methodological steps involved in interpreting qualitatively coded data in greater detail. For many scholars, interpretation 'happens wherever and whenever meaning is made' (Willig, 2014: 137) thereby 'creating a new narrative from the data' (Reyes et al., 2021: 6). When a researcher asks, 'what does this mean?', the number of answers can be unlimited as there exist variant ways to interpret the same thing. Thus, interpretation is always shaped by assumptions made by the researcher in the form of previous knowledge, personal preferences and the researcher's experience and background in terms of class, race, gender, (dis)ability and sexuality. It is also conditioned by what is, or is not, available in the data—i.e., own limitations. Put more directly, how we interpret our data is not only shaped by our positionality, but also by the epistemological and ontological views we harbour prior to embarking on the project of interpreting (for more on positionality, see Ackerly & True, 2020). Whilst interpretation can be shaped by the above factors, it can also simultaneously generate different types of knowledge, which means that researchers are responsible for assessing, criticising and restricting the generalisability of their findings (Lewis et al., 2003; Schwartz-Shea & Yanow, 2012).

As stated in previous chapters, different stages of qualitative research—such as data gathering and data coding—may be conducted at the level of the broader research project or at the level of research articles. In that sense, Chapter 4 showed that the document data was mainly selected to match the research design and questions of specific research articles, whilst interview and ethnographic data was gathered according to the broader objectives of the project. Similarly, Chapter 5 explained how we coded the interview and ethnographic data collaboratively using a coding strategy designed for the whole project, whereas document data was coded with a coding scheme designed for research articles. This chapter is exclusively attentive to the interpretation of data relative to research questions developed for the purpose of research articles, some as single-authored and others with up to six co-authors.[1]

---

[1] Forming part of the broader research project, all research articles had a research design consistent with the project objectives.

Qualitative research is often based on analyses that are driven by research questions (Blaikie, 2010; Schwartz-Shea & Yanow, 2012). We applied this approach so that all the questions asked in individual research articles matched the broader questions of the project. Likewise, all research articles contributed to the empirical, theoretical, and methodological findings of the broader project. The broad initial research questions of the project were: *'how does gender create fault lines between and within political groups?'*; *'how do gendered norms impact formal and informal practices in the EP?'*; and *'how are gendered policies and practices in the EP and the political groups shaped by political ideologies?'* Whilst these research questions informed particular articles (as overall research aims or goals), we sometimes had different—narrower or broader—aims and objectives in other publications.

Some research articles focused on the interpretation of frames and discourses used by political groups on specific policies. For example, when considering sexuality and human rights we asked, *'how do the political groups in the EP understand and (re)frame human rights?'* (Ahrens et al., 2022); on social and economic policies we asked, *'how is gender equality sidelined in the EP on EU economic governance'* (Elomäki, 2021); and *'how do dominant ideas in the EU's economic governance shape the constructions and frames of economic and social issues?'* (Elomäki & Gaweda, 2022); and on gendered violence we asked, *'how are sexual harassment, and solutions to it, discursively constructed in the EP by the political groups?'* (Berthet & Kantola, 2021); and *'how are support and opposition to the EU's ratification of the Istanbul Convention on violence against women and domestic violence constructed in the EP by the political groups?'* (Berthet, 2022a).

Other publications, however, focused on interpreting the formal and informal practices of the political groups. For example, in relation to the formation of political groups we asked, *'how are the formal and informal practices of political group formation gendered in the EP and what does it mean for democracy?'* (Ahrens & Kantola, 2022); in relation to Brexit we asked, *'how was the impact of Brexit constructed in the EP, and how did it affect UK MEPs' parliamentary work?'* (Kantola & Miller, 2023). When we considered the dynamics of intra-group policy formation, we asked, *'how do political groups formulate group lines on policies and how does it impact democratic decision-making in the EP and intra-group democracy?'* (Elomäki et al., 2022); and in relation to national party delegations (NPDs) we asked, *'how is the role of NPDs constructed within the political groups and what differences does this elicit between them? What formal and informal institutions are at play?'* (Elomäki et al., 2023). Finally, some research articles used the data in a different way, namely, not to interpret constructions, but rather to trace the development of a specific policy within the parliament. Good examples of this were the enquiry into the parliamentary process of the European Semester policy developments (Elomäki, 2021) and into those that led to the adoption of the Matić resolution on sexual and reproductive health and rights in Europe (Berthet, 2022b).

THE ROLE OF CODE REPORTS
IN INTERPRETATION AND ANALYSIS

The first step towards interpretation was to export the code report from ATLAS.ti. The previous chapter covered the details of coding qualitative data in ATLAS.ti, the different tools and functions offered by the software to code and become familiar with the data and to begin analysing it by employing labels, categories and revealing patterns. We regarded the step of exporting code reports as the first step of interpretation. As we explained in Chapter 5, a code report can retrieve all quotations from one code or several codes, or all quotations at the intersection of one or more code(s) and of one or more document(s). Once retrieved, the reports consist of pages of quotations from interviews or ethnographic notes; its length will depend on the total amount of data and the level of fine-grained analysis the researcher exporting the report is seeking.

First, we began by reading the code report, either as a whole or by dividing it amongst co-authors. If the publication is to be co-authored, the reports can be divided either by categories (e.g., team A reads political groups X; team B reads political groups Y; or team A reads female respondents; team B reads male respondents), or by sections of analysis planned in the research article (e.g., team A is assigned the part on informal practices and will read the data through that lens). Whilst reading the report is an individual task, it is imperative that regular meetings are scheduled to fully discuss this first stage of analysing the data with all co-authors.

Even if we divided the analytical work between team members, we often read whole interviews to ensure we did not 'take things out of context' or mistake the participants' meaning. This also depended on the research questions and led us to reflect on the limitations of team coding. With qualitative research, context and subtext are key for meaningful interpretation of the data and at times, limited quotations (coded by someone else) could be confusing. Our solution was for each team member to be as familiar as possible with all the relevant data that was used for any particular publication. We also used different types of data side-by-side (see Box 6.1 for an example), reinforcing our interpretation by using videos, debate transcripts and parliamentary documents. Depending on the type of article being produced, we could change the significance or weight of data we relied upon.

Box 6.1 Triangulating different data sources and using a different coding scheme

Elomäki and Gaweda (2022) developed a new coding scheme that corresponded to their specific research questions, because they used data that mostly consisted of EP committee documents. They triangulated the research material to juxtapose, compare and contrast the data from EP documents, debates and interviews, to enhance credibility and increase the validity of their interpretive outcomes. Specifically, they coded the document material in ATLAS.ti to structure the extensive data for discursive and interpretive textual analysis, and to allow for comparisons between committees and groups.

The coding system was developed deductively and inductively based on the literature attentive to the hierarchy between social and economic goals. They designed and discussed it in multiple meetings to ensure consistency and coherence between the coders. The coding system aimed to identify discursive constructions of the social-economic relationship (for example economy prioritised over social goals or the reverse), the specific social policy issues discussed (for example poverty, different care services, etc.) and discursive constructions of these issues (for example, as a cost, an investment, valuable in itself, applying labour market logic). In the case of this article, the authors also analysed videos of 20 committee debates corresponding to the reports, following a schedule of sensitising questions on political conflicts and policy content. The committee debates provided interpretive material for the analysis of the political and ideological context of the discourses. Finally, they only used the project interviews dataset to contextualise, explore meta-narratives and nuance within political group positions, and to gain insights into the policy-making processes (Elomäki & Gaweda, 2022).

Several factors combine to justify the need to co-author articles in qualitative research. Two of our research articles were co-authored by all six researchers involved in the project. One consisted of analysing the normative whiteness and racism in the European Parliament using the code 'Racism', and generated unforeseen research findings that exceeded the initial objectives of the project (Kantola et al., 2023). The other article involved the analysis of the power dynamics between national party delegations in the European Parliament. Co-authoring it as a whole team made sense, as the code 'National Party Delegations' was the biggest we had returning over 490 quotations. Thus, it was more efficient and logical to analyse the code with more researchers. For the latter publication, each researcher or group of two researchers was in charge of reading the 'National Party Delegation' code report for one big political group or two small political groups. After reading and extracting important parts of the text, joint discussions of findings (including patterns and differences) amongst all researchers were key to systematise and remain consistent with the analysis.

INTERPRETING FRAMES AND DISCOURSES

The analysis of qualitative data may involve the interpretation of frames and discourses prior to analysing policies and policy developments, formal and informal practices, and parliamentary processes. Epistemologically, we approached knowledge as constructed (Yanow, 2006a), thus the methodologies relevant to us were interpretivist and constructivist. The former relies on the belief that the analysis of human actions and practices is possible by interpreting the meanings that actors attribute to actions, practices, and the institutional environment in which they operate (Bevir, 2006: 283). Put simply, interpretative qualitative research is typically unconcerned with inferring or hypothesising the 'one and only' truth from the data, rather it is focused on analysing and attempting to understand the variant constructions that emerge from the data. For instance, when analysing the role and meaning of expertise in the European Parliament, researchers may not be interested in the subject and the object (i.e., the expert and the expertise), instead they will be attentive to who is *constructed as* an expert, what is *constructed as* expertise and how does it impact policy developments in parliaments (for an example of constructing expertise in the EP, see Elomäki & Haapala, 2023).

Similarly, when analysing the role and power of national delegations in the EP, our team was not interested in quantifying the power of national delegations, but rather in analysing which delegations were *constructed as* powerful and why (Elomäki et al., 2023). Thus, constructive and interpretative methodologies may involve questioning which discursive constructions are dominant, and which are silenced, in order to look for hegemonies, power dynamics and omissions. Rather than 'truths' or objective facts, interpretivist scholars tease out textual substance to be interpreted. With that in mind, scholars have argued that the attribution of meaning to actions, practices and to their institutional environment is best explored through an analysis of frames and discourses (Lindekilde, 2014)—which, in turn, are best understood using a qualitative toolkit (Bevir, 2006).

Although there exist a variety of ways to interpret frames and discourses, they are all concerned with how language (i.e., talk or text) constructs social realities (Willig, 2014), or to assert that discourses are socially constructed, and consequently play a predominant role in constituting the social (Blommaert & Bulcaen, 2000: 448). Interpretivist and constructivist methodologies acknowledge the constraints that broader discursive environments impose on individual discursive practices (Ferree et al., 2002). Language or discourse are not 'transparent tools' and thus require a significant degree of interpretation as to what is constructed and how (Bacchi, 1999). Therefore, one key site of analysis is the discursive battles over meanings that are played out between various actors, and the consideration of the constraints imposed by their institutional discursive environments (Lindekilde, 2014). In our case, this has meant, for instance, studying the discursive constructions around gendered policy issues, the differences and similarities between political groups, the fault lines within the groups and to embed/contrast those within broader discursive frames, such as the self-promoted narrative of championing gender equality in the European Parliament.

In our epistemological approach—which is interpretivist, constructivist but also often post-structural and feminist—we understand discourse as that which is infiltrated by power relations, because power is omnipresent and performative (Foucault, 1972, 1980). The post-structuralist approach in terms of discourse analysis emphasises both discursive and non-discursive elements of social reality, such as institutional practices and norms guiding behaviour (Panizza & Miorelli, 2013). Importantly, these are mutually constitutive, which allows for a fuller understanding of the role of discourse in creating power (and inequality). From this point of view, the social orders we observed in institutions were never fully structured, but they were open to political interventions and dislocations that made it possible to ground or subvert them (Panizza & Miorelli, 2013: 302). From our standpoint, social phenomena are not purely discursive or linguistic, but for things to be intelligible they must exist as part of a wider framework of meaning and discourse (cf. Fairclough, 1995; Jorgensen & Phillips, 2002; Panizza & Miorelli, 2013).

This reasoning is especially important when feminist methodology is an 'epistemology in action' (Weldon, 2006). Typically, a feminist perspective implies a critical approach, one aimed at creating social change or exposing social injustice and inequality. The position of the researcher, and individual choices in terms of methods whilst reflecting one's ontological and epistemological commitments, have implications in feminist research that differ markedly from traditional positivist social science. The approach moves beyond a determinist and traditionally positivist concept of causality, providing instead a reflexive perspective and a contextualised and dynamic way of interpreting meaning (Kulawik, 2009: 263). When combined, different forms of knowledge will arguably produce, not a claim to universal understanding, but rather a broader, albeit contingent, understanding of the nexus of gender, institutions, power and discourse in legislatures (Jorgensen & Phillips, 2002: 155).

In other words, making sense of how discourses maintain, challenge and transform (unequal) power relations within a given institution (Fairclough, 1995; Wodak, 1996), is a critical approach to the analysis of discourse (Willig, 2014). Discourse can be seen as a form of social practice that both constitutes the social world and is constituted by other social practices. '[T]he discursive constitution of society does not emanate from a free play of ideas in people's heads, but from social practice which is firmly rooted in and oriented in real, material and social structures' (Fairclough, 1992: 66). Thus, the ability to define social realities by making one discourse or frame dominant 'is an act of power with important consequences for social practices' (Lindekilde, 2014: 199).

In gender and politics scholarship, this has meant conceptualising social structures, such as gendered inequalities, as cemented by power relations

(Kantola & Lombardo, 2017). A feminist approach to (critical) discourse analysis cannot remain descriptive and neutral, since the interests guiding it aim to uncover or make transparent processes and mechanisms that perpetuate injustice, inequality, manipulation, sexual discrimination in both overt and subtle, pernicious forms (Sunderland & Litosseliti, 2002: 20). Therefore, analysing the discursive layers embedded in institutions can help understand the processes through which power moulds these institutions in the form they take (Sunderland & Litosseliti, 2002). In this regard, discursive practices influence what can be said, achieved and reformed in an institution (Bacchi, 2009; Lombardo et al., 2009). Critical frame analysis is an additional tool for analysing discourses. It calls for reflection on both the discourses within which actors operate, and the active deployment of concepts and categories for political purposes (Verloo, 2005; Verloo & Lombardo, 2007). A framing methodology shows the ways in which the framing of a concept or policy affects how policymakers and legislators think about an issue (Forest & Lombardo, 2012). Such methodologies are useful for interpreting the discourses and frames around policies or policy developments in parliaments.

Whilst there are similarities between discourse and frame analysis, they can be used to answer different research questions by identifying the different meanings a concept holds (Bacchi, 2009; Lindekilde, 2014; Lombardo & Meier, 2008; Lombardo et al., 2009; Roggeband & Verloo, 2006; Verloo, 2007). This is best illustrated for our purposes, through the ways in which gender equality is a disputed concept. Born out of social movement studies, frame analysis seeks to identify 'how particular ideas/ideology are used deliberately to mobilise supporters and demobilise adversaries vis-à-vis a particular goal' (Lindekilde, 2014: 200; Snow & Benford, 1988). It is used in other scholarship to analyse the strategic framings of a particular problem. For Bacchi (2009), problematising a policy issue leads neither to an objective description of it, nor to objective solutions for solving it. Rather, it is part of creating the problem. A framing methodology shows the ways in which the framing of a concept affects how policymakers and legislators think about an issue.

Previous research on the European Parliament uses interviews as data to gain 'objective' information (as insights or direct records) on what had happened behind closed doors, such as in committee negotiations or in trilogues (Bressanelli & Chelotti, 2018; Ripoll Servant & Panning, 2019). Whilst our main focus was on discourses and framings, we also used the qualitative data to trace policy processes, analyse policy-making practices and identify obstacles for the promotion of gender equality within the political groups and in the European Parliament. For instance, some of our research was driven by the question *why pro-gender-equality amendments made by progressive political groups and MEPs often disappeared throughout the committee negotiation process?* Interviews with MEPs and staff from different political groups who were involved in negotiations about the specific reports, helped us to identify some of the dynamics that led to the sidelining of gender equality. Gender equality was not necessarily a priority for pro-equality groups in the negotiations, and it was opposed by some groups. Moreover, some of the political groups that made amendments about gender equality did not have enough leverage in the negotiations to push their views through, or may not have invested their resources on negotiation about reports they know will be voted against (Elomäki, 2021).

Policy and Process Tracing

In the policy-focused articles, we used the interview data as information to trace policy processes and policy-making practices. Whilst not looking for causality, or indeed to make claims about it, we used policy process tracing as a complementary method, or an additional level, to fully understand and interpret the discursive and non-discursive elements. As such we traced, outlined and connected the stages of a particular process, which enabled us to identify the power hierarchies, interplay of different formal and informal norms and the contingent reasons for the emergence of gendered inequalities in both institutional policy and practice. For instance, since some interview participants were experts on economic issues, either as MEPs, political group staff or committee staff and represented a fair balance of political groups, we used this approach to study the development of economic policies in the parliament. For those experts, the interview questions were highly specific and delved deeper into the specificities of some policy processes. This approach elicited rich and multifaceted knowledge about parliamentary processes, boosting our within-case analysis. However, we also experienced the well-documented difficulties of using interviews as sources of 'objective' information. Indeed, in an interview narrative the unfolding of events may be influenced by memory effects, unwillingness to answer questions, strategic misrepresentation of events and the tendency of actors to under—or over-represent some events or their own role in them (e.g., Berry, 2002; Beyers et al., 2014; Fowler et al., 2011).

Not surprisingly, it became evident that most of our interviewees wanted to present themselves and their political groups in a favourable light. Concomitantly, they were not necessarily ready to provide sensitive information. For instance, our data related to the moment when two MEPs had come to an agreement for a committee position on a specific file and represented themselves as winners of negotiations. They omitted to mention, however, the dissatisfaction of the coordinators in the outcome—as stressed by other interviewees who took part in the policy process. Similarly, our data stressed a number of contradictory accounts amongst interviewees in relation to policy-making processes at play in the political groups, with some interviewees describing how everyone's opinion is allowed, whilst others from the same group stressed the silencing of dissenting voices. Such contradictions show the difficulty of using interviews as accurate evidence about the unfolding of events.

Therefore, even when asking research questions about processes and practices, we acknowledge that interviews do not provide access to an 'objective' reality, but are always a construction based on perceptions. Interview data can certainly point one in a certain direction to find out more, but it needs to be complemented with other sources to obtain a fuller picture whilst simultaneously addressing possible biases in the data (Natow, 2020). At the same time, our commitment to interpretivist, constructivist and feminist qualitative epistemological research, ensured that claims or assumptions of reaching 'objective' truths or determining causality, were never made (Yanow, 2006b). Unlike positivist empirical methods designed to generate results that can be replicated by different scholars, interpretivist, constructivist and feminist can yield different outcomes in the hands of different researchers. This highlights the collective self-reflective and deliberative nature of such approaches (Ackerly et al., 2006: 7).

To counterbalance the limitations of interview data, we triangulated it with document data, such as parliamentary debates, amendments and political group documents—thus providing a more complete grasp on specific policy processes (see Box 6.1 above for an example; for more on triangulation, see Natow, 2020). This helped with cross-validating and interpreting the evidence obtained through interviews, and allowed for the integration of additional information (Beyers et al., 2014). In turn, ethnographic data provided an additional important tool to analyse the practices of political groups, enriching our knowledge of parliamentary practices and policy processes.

INTERPRETING ETHNOGRAPHIC DATA

Because ethnographic fieldnotes are subjective, even personal, and sometimes written down in conditions not always conducive to note-taking, the generated data is by its nature difficult to share with other researchers for analysis. For the ethnographer, this meant several difficult and thorough rounds of rewriting fieldnotes to make them intelligible to others (Jarzabkowski et al., 2014). In this respect, it was important to establish a protocol, shared with all other researchers in the team, that structured the process of taking field notes (see Chapter 3 for the template), and which allowed us to co-author research articles with our ethnographer. Overall, we took a structured approach to the analysis of fieldnotes.

There are different ways of interpreting and presenting evidence from ethnographic data (Cerwonka & Malkki, 2007; Schatz, 2009; Shore et al., 2011), and this is further reflected in the variant scholarship that employs parliamentary ethnography (Abélès, 1993; Crewe, 2018; Miller, 2022). Like interview data, the analysis of ethnographic data occurs across different research stages and is influenced by decisions made at various moments. For example, designing the research idea, formulating the questions, deciding on a protocol to record fieldwork interactions and writing down fieldnotes. Whilst it is important to avoid making 'instant interpretations' in order 'to remain as reflexive as possible' (Niemi, 2010: 89), Ackerly and True note that the process of ethnographic data production and analysis are inextricably linked (2020: 190). Sometimes, the goal is to open up the black boxes of what is little known or understudied to produce a thick description.

In our case, the analysis of ethnographic data was abductive and nonlinear. It can be referred to as both a formal and an informal process. The process was formal because it took shape in analytic notes and memoranda, and it was informal because it was embodied in the ethnographer's 'ideas and hunches' (Hammersley & Atkinson, 2019: 167). For instance, we used informal strategies, such as 'hanging around' with research participants, to discuss research ideas and test whether they resonated with them. Such informality can generate shared understandings with research participants, bring about new perspectives, or be shut down at once.

We included ethnographic analytic notes or memos into the fieldnotes, either as appendages at the bottom, or weaved them through the text when writing them up, but we acknowledge that they can be written in a separate document. In terms of the formal placing of the analysis amongst the fieldnotes, we eventually wrote the analytic notes and fieldwork diary in conjunction and merged them as 'raw' data. The observation protocol included a section for 'reflections', in which the ethnographer reflected on the observation just made (see Box 6.2 for examples). The ethnographer noted their positionality in the observation protocol, though they were inevitably present in the whole field note as they were noting the dynamics that they saw as relevant. In other political ethnographies, ethnographers have one column of 'raw' fieldnotes and then an analysis column, or if handwritten they write with a different pen.

Box 6.2 Ideas for prompts in analytical ethnographic notes

(1) Using **references to literature** and ideas from the 'raw' data: for instance when a participant mentions topics that make the researcher think, or academic literature they read on the issue, even using random associations.

(2) Discussing **emerging interpretative ideas** with research participants, for instance 'running them by' field members to see if they resonate in informal conversations or settings.

(3) Documenting one's own **surprises** about observations in the field: noting down researcher's own emotional reactions and reflecting later why that happened.

(4) Documenting **the research process in terms of theoretical sampling:** for instance, trying to get an interview with interpreters or other field participants, who might otherwise be seen as 'bystanders' in the political processes. This is useful to discuss affective dynamics, since the interpreters, for example, implied to us that they sensed the mood of group meetings. Interestingly, some interpreters interpret empathetically, becoming key agents in palpably gauging the mood in the room, which is valuable when looking into affects and affective atmospheres.

(5) **Comparing** shadowing experiences from the locations of two differently situated participants that might be working within the same group and committee to discern patterns and divergences.

(6) Marking **links to other sources** to triangulate ethnographic fieldnotes, either using the interview dataset or own observations in the field—notes, for example, about the location, posters, images and embodiment.

(7) **Comparing unusual** (crisis) **situational contexts** with 'normal' contexts: for instance, when unexpected circumstances affect regular institutional procedures. In our case, it was the onset of the Covid-19 pandemic and announced restrictions to the EP President's conference. We noted how exceptionally open Sassoli's press conference was for ordinary people in the parliament.

(8) **Situating parliamentary powers**: in the notes it is useful to reflect on the institutional context the researcher is studying, and to compare it with other political institutions they know along power relationship lines, especially in similar circumstances—how, for example, does the president of the EP behave relative to a national parliamentary speaker?

As mentioned previously, ethnographic scholars debate the possibility of sharing ethnographic data with other researchers for interpretation (Murphy et al., 2021; Reyes, 2018; Tsai et al., 2016). When ethnographers of parliaments consider sharing their fieldnotes data, two difficulties are often raised: (1) the long-standing feeling that data is 'hard won and the result of personal, trusting relationships' built over years—which requires time away from the desk and less opportunities to craft findings into publications; and (2) the lack of full control over confidentiality and anonymity required when citing ethnographic data in research articles, when this was key to the trust built with participants (Murphy et al., 2021; Tsai et al., 2016). For this reason, our ethical statement specifically included the requirement to not harm research participants—which in ethnography with elite participants may mean not harming their political career. Furthermore, although metadata about the fieldnotes was included, we shared the fieldnotes with the team and co-authors, though not more widely. Murphy et al. (2021) do offer practical solutions, such as placing an embargo on data, and going back to subjects to ask them if they consent to archiving their stories.

With regard to the practicalities of presenting ethnographic data, we often used it as 'raw data' in research articles, but other ways of presenting ethnographic evidence that conveys dynamics of parliamentary worlds include vignettes, composite narratives that link together several actors and interactions from the field, and more temporal 'process' narratives (Jarzabkowski et al., 2014). In the course of our analyses, we also searched the ethnographic field notes for dissenting voices. This was especially important in the case of publications on more 'invisible' and problematic issues, like the article on institutional racism and normative whiteness in the European Parliament (Kantola et al., 2023).

Ethnographic data allowed us also to interpret wider facets of parliamentary institutional behaviour and norms than documents or interviews alone would have permitted. Thanks to specific codes we developed to capture affects and emotions, we were able to interpret the use of strong language and figures, 'affective atmospheres' (as more collective emotional entities rather than just a person expressing a feeling), as well as the observation of 'tense' or 'businesslike' interactions in meeting or encounters in our research articles (Kantola & Miller, 2021: 788). For instance, in their article on the affective impact of Brexit in the EP, Kantola and Miller (2023) did not measure the effectiveness of parliamentary work or politicians' motivations and performance, but rather analysed its dimensions. Specifically, they covered the influence of emotion and affect on the constructions of parliamentary work, finding that these constructions were charged with emotions including sadness, joy, hope, civilised jubilation, relief, resolve and vigilance and that these were expressed and controlled (Kantola & Miller, 2023). The findings were largely based on the ethnographic material and contribute to studies on parliamentary work by moving away from more positivist and rational choice versions of role theory and categorising the roles of parliamentarians, to mapping how they construct different dimensions of parliamentary work (Kantola & Miller, 2023), thereby demonstrating the 'added value' of utilising ethnographic data.

CONCLUSION

This chapter finalised our section on analysing qualitative data by casting a critical eye over the epistemological and methodological steps of interpretation. Whilst many different ways to analyse qualitative material exist, we were attentive to the important aspects involved with the interpretation of qualitative data, in particular, how it is shaped by the researcher's own positionality and epistemological and ontological disposition. These factors serve to generate different types of knowledge, meaning that qualitative researchers are required to assess, criticise and restrict the generalisability of their findings. The interpretation of qualitative data is typically driven by research questions. In our case, this has meant interpreting frames and discourses, analysing formal and informal practices, tracing policy processes and policy-making practices and interpreting ethnographic data. Whilst interpreting frames and discourses involved identifying different constructions that emerged from the data, and analysing them via interpretivist, constructivist, post-structuralist and feminist methodologies, tracing policy processes and policy-making practices significantly helped to identify power hierarchies, the interplay of different formal and informal norms as well as the emergence of gendered inequalities both in policies and practices. Finally, we have discussed the benefits and limitations of sharing ethnographic material and interpreting it for analysis. A difficult process eased by the use of ethnographic analytic notes or memos, fieldwork diaries and an observation protocol that reflected on the ethnographer's positionality.

REFERENCES

Abélès, M. (1993). Political anthropology of the trans-national institution: The European Parliament. *French Politics & Society, 11*(1), 1–19.
Ackerly, B., & True, J. (2020). *Doing feminist research in political and social science* (2nd ed.). Palgrave Macmillan.
Ackerly, B. A., Stern, M., & True, J. (2006). Feminist methodologies for international relations. In B. A. Ackerly, M. Stern, & J. True (Eds.), *Feminist methodologies for international relations* (pp. 1–16). Cambridge University Press.
Ahrens, P., & Kantola, J. (2022). Political group formation in the European parliament: Negotiating democracy and gender. *Party Politics, 0*(0). https://doi.org/10.1177/13540688221106295

Ahrens, P., Gaweda, B., & Kantola, J. (2022). Reframing the language of human rights? Political group contestations on women's and LGBTQI rights in European Parliament debates. *Journal of European Integration, 44*(6), 803–819.

Bacchi, C. (1999). *Women, policy and politics. The construction of policy problems.* Sage Publications.

Bacchi, C. (2009). *Analysing policy: What's the problem represented to be?* Pearson Higher Education.

Berry, J. M. (2002). Validity and reliability issues in elite interviewing. *Political Science & Politics, 35*(4), 679–682.

Berthet, V. (2022a). Norm under fire: Support for and opposition to the European Union's ratification of the Istanbul Convention in the European Parliament. *International Feminist Journal of Politics, 24*(5), 675–698.

Berthet, V. (2022b). United in crisis: Abortion politics in the European Parliament and political groups' disputes over EU values. *Journal of Common Market Studies, 60*(6), 1797–1814.

Berthet, V., & Kantola, J. (2021). Gender, violence, and political institutions: Struggles over sexual harassment in the European Parliament. *Social Politics, 28*(1), 143–167.

Bevir, M. (2006). How narratives explain. In P. Schwartz-Shea & D. Yanow (Eds.), *Interpretive research design: Concepts and processes* (pp. 281–290). Taylor & Francis.

Beyers, J., Braun, C., Marshall, D., & De Bruycker, I. (2014). Let's talk! On the practice and method of interviewing policy experts. *Interest Groups & Advocacy, 3,* 174–187.

Blaikie, N. (2010). *Designing social research* (2nd ed.). Polity Press.

Blommaert, J., & Bulcaen, C. (2000). Critical discourse analysis. *Annual Reviews Publishers, 29,* 447–466.

Bressanelli, E., & Chelotti, N. (2018). The European Parliament and economic governance: Explaining a case of limited influence. *The Journal of Legislative Studies, 24*(1), 72–89.

Cerwonka, A., & Malkki, L. H. (2007). *Improvising theory: Process and temporality in ethnographic fieldwork.* University of Chicago Press.

Crewe, E. (2018). Ethnographies of parliament: Culture and uncertainty in shallow democracies. *Journal of Organizational Ethnography, 7*(1), 16–30.

Elomäki, A. (2021). "It's a total no-no": The strategic silence about gender in the European Parliament's economic governance policies. *International Political Science Review, 0*(0), https://doi.org/10.1177/019251212097832

Elomäki, A., & Gaweda, B. (2022). Looking for the 'social' in the European semester: The ambiguous 'socialisation' of EU economic governance in the European Parliament. *Journal of Contemporary European Research, 18*(1), 166–183.

Elomäki, A., & Haapala, T. (2023). *Constructing expertise in the European Parliament. Democratic legitimacy and political actors.* Paper presented at the seminar on researching the European Union, 1 March 2023, University of Helsinki, Finland.

Elomäki, A., Gaweda, B., & Berthet, V. (2022). Democratic practices and political dynamics of intra-group policy formation in the European Parliament. In P. Ahrens, A. Elomäki, & J. Kantola (Eds.), *European Parliament's political groups in turbulent times* (pp. 73–96). Springer International Publishing.

Elomäki, A., Kantola, J., Ahrens, P., Berthet, V., Gaweda, B., & Miller, C. (2023). *The politics of national delegations in the European Parliament.* Paper presented at the Center for European Studies (CES) seminar on researching the European Union, 1 February 2023, University of Helsinki, Finland.

Fairclough, N. (1992). *Discourse and social change.* Polity Press.

Fairclough, N. (1995). *Critical discourse analysis.* Longman.

Ferree, M. M., Gamson, W. A., Gerhards, J., & Rucht, D. (2002). *Shaping abortion discourse: Democracy and the public sphere in Germany and the United States.* Cambridge University Press.

Forest, M., & Lombardo, E. (2012). *The Europeanization of gender equality policies: A discursive-sociological approach.* Palgrave Macmillan.

Foucault, M. (1972). *The archeology of knowledge.* Tavistock.

Foucault, M. (1980). *Power/knowledge. Selected interviews and other writings 1972–1977 by Michel Foucault.* Prentice Hall.

Fowler, J. H., Heaney, M. T., Nickerson, D. W., Padgett, J. F., & Sinclair, B. (2011). Causality in political networks. *American Politics Research, 39*(2), 437–480.

Hammersley, M., & Atkinson, P. (2019). *Ethnography principles in practice.* Routledge.

Jarzabkowski, P., Bednarek, R., & Le, K. (2014). Producing persuasive findings: De-mystifying ethnographic textwork in strategy and organization research. *Strategic Organization, 12*(4), 274–287.

Jorgensen, M., & Phillips, L. (2002). *Discourse analysis as theory and method.* Sage Publications.

Kantola, J., & Lombardo, E. (2017). *Gender and political analysis.* Bloomsbury Publishing.

Kantola, J., & Miller, C. (2021). Party politics and radical right populism in the European Parliament: Analysing political groups as democratic actors. *Journal of Common Market Studies, 59*(4), 782–801.

Kantola, J., & Miller, C. (2023). Eternal friends or jubilant Brexiteers? The impact of Brexit on UK MEPs' parliamentary work in the European Parliament. *Journal of Common Market Studies, 61,* 712–729.

Kantola, J., Elomäki, A., Gaweda, B., Miller, C., Ahrens, P., & Berthet, V. (2023). "It's like shouting to a brick wall": Normative whiteness and racism in the European Parliament. *American Political Science Review, 117*(1), 184–199.

Kulawik, T. (2009). Staking the frame of a feminist discursive institutionalism. *Politics & Gender, 5*(2), 262–271.

Lewis, J., Ritchie, J., Ormston, R., & Morrell, G. (2003). *Qualitative research practice: A guide for social science students and researchers*. Sage Publications.

Lindekilde, L. (2014). Discourse and frame analysis: In-depth analysis of qualitative data in social movement research. In D. della Porta (Ed.), *Methodological practices in social movement research* (pp. 195–227). Oxford University Press.

Lombardo, E., & Meier, P. (2008). Framing gender equality in the European Union political discourse. *Social Politics, 15*(1), 101–129.

Lombardo, E., Meier, P., & Verloo, M. (Eds.). (2009). *The discursive politics of gender equality: Stretching, bending and policy-making*. Routledge.

Miller, C. (2022). 'Ethno, ethno, what?': Using ethnography to explore the European Parliament's political groups in turbulent times. In *European Parliament's political groups in turbulent times* (pp. 245–266). Springer International Publishing.

Murphy, A. K., Jerolmack, C., & Smith, D. (2021). Ethnography, data transparency, and the information age. *Annual Review of Sociology, 47*, 41–61.

Natow, R. S. (2020). The use of triangulation in qualitative studies employing elite interviews. *Qualitative Research, 20*(2), 160–173.

Niemi, H. (2010). *Managing in the 'golden cage': An ethnographic study of work, management and gender in parliamentary administration*. Ph.D. thesis submitted to Hanken School of Economics, Helsinki.

Panizza, F., & Miorelli, R. (2013). Taking discourse seriously: Discursive institutionalism and post-structuralist discourse theory. *Political Studies, 61*(2), 301–318.

Reyes, V. (2018). Three models of transparency in ethnographic research: Naming places, naming people, and sharing data. *Ethnography, 19*(2), 204–226.

Reyes, V., Bogumil, E., & Welch, L. E. (2021). The living codebook: Documenting the process of qualitative data analysis. *Sociological Methods & Research, 0*(0). https://doi.org/10.1177/0049124120986185

Ripoll Servent, A., & Panning, L. (2019). Eurosceptics in trilogue settings: Interest formation and contestation in the European Parliament. *West European Politics, 42*(4), 755–775.

Roggeband, C., & Verloo, M. (2006). Evaluating gender impact assessment in the Netherlands (1994–2004): A political process approach. *Policy & Politics, 34*(4), 615–632.

Schatz, E. (2009). *Political ethnography: What immersion contributes to the study of power*. Chicago University Press.

Schwartz-Shea, P., & Yanow, D. (2012). *Interpretive research design: Concepts and processes.* Taylor & Francis.

Shore, C., Wright, S., & Peró, D. (2011). *Policy worlds: Anthropology and the analysis of contemporary power.* Berghahn Books.

Snow, D. A., & Benford, R. D. (1988). Ideology, frame resonance, and participant mobilization. *International Social Movement Research, 1*(1), 197–217.

Sunderland, J., & Litosseliti, L. (2002). *Gender identity and discourse analysis. Discourse approaches to politics, society, and culture.* John Benjamins Publishing.

Tsai, A. C., Kohrt, B. A., Matthews, L. T., Betancourt, T. S., Lee, J. K., Papachristos, A. V., Weiser, S. D., & Dworkin, S. L. (2016). Promises and pitfalls of data sharing in qualitative research. *Social Science & Medicine, 169*, 191–198.

Verloo, M. (2005). Mainstreaming gender equality in Europe. A critical frame analysis approach. *The Greek Review of Social Research, 17*, 11–34.

Verloo, M. M. T., & Lombardo, E. (2007). Contested gender equality and policy variety in Europe: Introducing a critical frame analysis approach. In M. Verloo (Ed.), *Multiple meanings of gender equality: A critical frame analysis of gender policies in Europe* (pp. 21–49). Central European University Press.

Weldon, L. S. (2006). Inclusion and understanding: A collective methodology for feminist international relations. In B. A. Ackerly, M. Stern, & J. True (Eds.), *Feminist methodologies for international relations* (pp. 62–88). Cambridge University Press.

Willig, C. (2014). Interpretation and analysis. In U. Flick (Ed.), *The SAGE handbook of qualitative data analysis* (pp. 136–150). Sage Publications.

Wodak, R. (1996). *Disorders of discourse.* Longman.

Yanow, D. (2006a). Thinking interpretively: Philosophical presuppositions and the human sciences. In P. Schwartz-Shea & D. Yanow (Eds.), *Interpretation and methods: Empirical research methods and the interpretive turn* (2nd ed., pp. 5–26). M.E. Sharpe.

Yanow, D. (2006b). Neither rigorous nor objective? Interrogating criteria for knowledge claims in interpretative science. In P. Schwartz-Shea & D. Yanow (Eds.), *Interpretation and methods: Empirical research methods and the interpretive turn* (2nd ed., pp. 97–119). M.E. Sharpe.

CHAPTER 7

Conclusions

Abstract Beyond summarising the core themes of the book, namely that of reflecting on qualitative research in parliament; research collaboration, expertise-sharing and project management; as well as assessing the practices to make qualitative research known to and accessible to actors in the European Parliament, the concluding chapter is an open-ended discussion on the future venues for qualitative research in political institutions generally and the European Parliament more specifically. We discuss the epistemic benefits of how our research adds to and/or challenges the 'traditional' political science approaches. In conclusion, we also provide a thorough and transparent discussion of what we would do differently from the perspective of time. We conclude by proposing what could be next for qualitative research in the European Parliament. For instance, we debate both the potential for new legislative and institutional powers as well as future crises inevitably bringing issues in terms of research topics and access. Finally, we stress the informality of many procedures, practices and mechanisms we witnessed and discuss its meaning for transparency and democracy.

Keywords Assessment · Epistemic benefits · Retrospection · Future research

© The Author(s) 2023
V. Berthet et al., *Guide to Qualitative Research in Parliaments*,
https://doi.org/10.1007/978-3-031-39808-7_7

INTRODUCTION

This volume has provided a hands-on, step-by-step guide on doing qualitative research in parliaments. The discussion has been based on our own experiences of conducting a large-scale qualitative study in one supranational parliament—the European Parliament. Based on that experience, we formulated concrete pointers to overcoming obstacles and challenges faced by qualitative researchers studying parliaments. For us, the European Parliament constituted a unique environment and a larger field in which the gendered practices, processes and policy outputs of the political groups were situated. Throughout the book, we have explored the practical achievements and drawbacks that relate to the collaborative gathering and analysis of dense qualitative data (interviews, ethnography and documents) with an international team of six researchers at various career stages.

As a guide, this book has provided approaches and unique insights to conducting qualitative methodologies in the form of seven chapters each tailored to deal with a specific step of the research process. Its practical and illustrative approach answers questions such as *how to gather a large-scale qualitative data-set of interview, ethnographic, and document data in a parliamentary environment? How to handle raw data through storing and coding? How to make sense of coded data? How to transform qualitative data gathered and coded collectively into findings for single- or co-authored articles?* In this concluding chapter, we provide an overview of the main points developed in the book. We reflect on our methodological choices, on what we would do differently, and finally we discuss the potential trajectory of qualitative research in the study of parliaments.

REFLECTIONS ON QUALITATIVE RESEARCH IN PARLIAMENTS

In comparison to other methodologies, qualitative approaches pose different research questions about parliaments and their activities than positivist and quantitative studies do. This book has presented the main advantages of conducting qualitative research in parliaments. It highlighted the usefulness of such an approach for the better understanding of the everyday dimensions shaping democratic practices and policy-making in parliaments, whilst also providing concrete, user-friendly advice on how to conduct such research in practical terms. For example, rather than asking and measuring *what impact far-right groups have had in parliaments*; it might ask: *how do parliamentary actors experience the impact of far-right groups in parliaments?* Likewise, enquiring *how sexual harassment in parliaments is understood by parliamentary actors and what they understand as best ways of preventing it* may replace or coincide with measuring its frequency and impact. Thus, applying qualitative research to the study of parliaments advances knowledge on policy constructions, internal practices and processes that shape parliamentary work; whilst quantitative analyses of roll-call voting typically overlook relevant aspects about interpreting these votes, such as analysing how they are understood, and exploring the processes and informal dimensions that led to them. Interpretive research questions, as shown in this book, provide thicker descriptions and investigate how parliamentary actors make sense of parliamentary activity.

When it comes to assessing parliaments with regard to their gender equality policies and practices (understood intersectionally), the use of dichotomous or binary variables measured in formal indicators (such as sex or age seen as not interrelated categories) as is often the case in quantitative research, does not capture complexity and can often create progress bias. Qualitative research, on the other hand, challenges the illusion of progress in relation to equalities, and highlights the practices and processes that reproduce gendered and racialised inequalities. Meanwhile, interview environments can be overly controlled and unnatural, not capturing everyday factors affecting parliamentary actors' constructions, behaviours, or experiences. As shown in this guide, qualitative research is typically designed to capture the complexity of parliamentary life and work whilst reflecting on the nuances and limitations of the methodology itself.

Rather than measuring variables, we captured affective atmospheres in parliaments, and rather than measuring frequencies, we explored the variant discursive constructions of policy issues by parliamentary actors and analysed them through interpretive methodologies. This required solid and transparent strategies, but also constant reflection on what conditioned that knowledge and the replicability and generalisation possibilities of it. For instance, insights gained from ethnography allowed us to question the specifics of parliamentary activity, which generated actual concrete examples, rather than generalised statements.

Whilst qualitative methodologies tend to provide rich and varied datasets, the gathering and analysis of them can be immensely time and resource consuming. We have given this book a strong focus on collaborations and sharing expertise because we believe it is what made the handling of dense qualitative data possible. Sharing the expertise and burden of data gathering, coding and of data interpretation can be a key strategy to handle big qualitative datasets in a timely fashion, and geared towards publication outputs.

However, as we consistently mentioned throughout the book, such a collaborative approach demands strict organisation and a high level of transparency and trust between the researchers. For instance, we found that clear and standardised labelling of data and formally designated people overseeing each task was a good organisational strategy. Furthermore, sharing the workload sometimes included outsourcing different tasks, such as interview transcriptions, which was only possible thanks to generous funding. Rather than listing instructions on how to conduct qualitative research in parliaments, this book, as suggested in the title, has offered some ideas to *guide* other researchers in this endeavour. Without doubt, there are things we would do differently.

HINDSIGHT: WHAT WOULD WE DO DIFFERENTLY?

When conducting qualitative research, one of the main concerns involves gathering data that is sufficiently representative of the field. In our case, a better cross-section of nationality representation mattered as our field was a multi-national parliament. On this aspect, we could have had a stronger representation of some nationalities, which was often made impossible or difficult because of language barriers or accessibility/availability issues. Some of these challenges may have been resolved if we could have allocated more resources to alleviate language obstacles and reach more non-English speakers. For instance, we could have offered an interpreter for participants from un(der)represented member states. Likewise, we could have explored ways to integrate the insights of hard to reach groups in parliament, such as staff hired for catering, cleaning and maintenance services who—in the case of the European Parliament—are contractually more vulnerable, French-speaking, have less flexibility with their working day and limited experiences of participating in research interviews. At the same time, this would have demanded different ethical considerations, as we would have asked for time and contributions from people who are not remunerated on a par with other employees of the European Parliament. We would also need to reflect on what use we would be to the more vulnerable employees and what our research could improve in a normative sense. Even though we found interview and ethnographic data to be highly useful in answering questions about discursive constructions as well as formal and informal practices of parliamentary work, we found, retrospectively, that a 'solid' pool of official documents from political groups helped us to cross-check the details and intricacies of processes. For example, guidelines for new parliamentarians and harassment policies. These may not be accessible online, but can be obtained through informal contacts in parliament. This takes time and demands a pro-active, reaching-out attitude and requires knowledge of who is in possession of such documents and might be willing to share them.

As the discussion in Chapter 6 illustrated, there are obstacles to using interviews as 'objective' sources of information, especially when considering the risks of memory alteration when recollecting events, and the tendency of actors to under—or over-represent some events and/or their own role in them (e.g., Berry, 2002; Beyers et al., 2014; Fowler et al., 2011). In this sense, documents can help to cross-check information gathered via interviewing. Having several ethnographers in the research team may also be an asset, especially as it allows for a more diverse representation of activities. For example, a lot of parliamentary meetings are held simultaneously, which means that prioritisations have to be made when scheduling observing activities.

In recent years, Twitter and other social media platforms have become a significant aspect of parliamentary activity and parliaments themselves are moving towards the idea of 'smart parliaments' (Fitsilis & Mikros, 2022). Concomitantly, there is greater acknowledgement that politicians and parliamentarians have integrated all kinds of social media in their daily activities, both for sharing information and for surveying their popularity. In that sense, we recognise that gathering digital data has become an important part of research, including qualitative research, but has mostly remained outside the scope of our research.

With regard to data analysis and especially coding, we could have also explored some innovative forms of coding, as detailed in recent textbooks (Saldana, 2021). For example, the analysis of ethnographic data could also include process codes, meaning the codes that highlight what parliamentary actors were doing during observations. Furthermore, coding can quickly become routine and less analytical or precise. In that sense, even though Chapter 5 stressed the importance of communicating transparently, there are always more opportunities for team debriefing. For instance, interactive and collaborative platforms such as Padlet, provide a forum for asynchronous communication. This facilitates ways in which multi-member research teams could share posts as ideas arise in the excitable process of coding, as well as in more general periods of reflection outside the formal coding process. Such forums may be seen as more digital and interactive versions of the research diaries or memos presented in this book.

By its nature, and epistemological orientation, qualitative research and especially ethnography require a large degree of improvisation, borne largely from the timing constraints of parliamentarians, as well as sometimes interpreting and exercising the autonomy provided by a parliamentary pass on a study visit. It is therefore important to establish a presence in the parliament. Practices to achieve this can include: an active project website and Twitter account; an identifiable project logo; clear, user-friendly documents on the research project such as information sheets and interview schedules, posters advertising events (displayed in the parliament) and roundtable co-operation from parliamentarians at events who might repost the details of the event for further publicity and invite and alert their networks to researchers' presence. Although these tactics are not enough, and can be swiftly weakened by unexpected events, such as the Covid-19 pandemic, we also acknowledge that research findings remain largely disseminated in the English language, providing a de facto limit to the possibilities of sharing knowledge more widely.

Knowledge exchange can also make qualitative research known to and accessible to actors within and without parliaments. Whilst there was some spillover to the practitioner world (Warasin et al., 2020), knowledge exchange was not a priority for our research funder. Different funders and universities might have different expectations, as well as the expertise and infrastructure for such activities. A follow-up activity is to measure any benefits accrue as a result of sharing research findings, such as changing understandings within or about parliament, or catalysing action going forward within parliaments. Whilst researchers in majoritarian parliaments are cautiously warned not to align oneself with a particular tribe (Crewe, 2021), parliaments that are not organised along majoritarian lines might provide more flexible opportunities to share knowledge with different groups.

Looking Ahead: Where Next for Qualitative Research on Parliaments?

A future academic endeavour that promises much interest, would be a state-of-the-art study on the types of qualitative methods that have been used in parliaments, where, and with what epistemic effects. This would provide this exciting field of study with a synthetic and comprehensive perspective on 'what's already out there'. For instance, it might provide more nuanced insight into how focus groups are underrepresented in the methodological literature on political institutions and parliaments (possibly due to time and linguistic constraints). Meta-level academic reflections, and further debate on the types of data that qualitative methods produce in parliaments are needed, as well as discussions about what implications these have for researchers' normative positions on social justice, gender equality and the fairness and equity of representation of own-voices.

On a more practical level, the qualitative research of parliaments may be affected by emerging challenges, if not crises, within and external to parliaments. Parliamentary crises, and the politicisation of policy areas and practices, inevitably bring about topical and thematic issues in terms of research subjects and access to them. In the case of the European Parliament, examples include the 'Qatar scandal' that has foregrounded and exposed a lack of transparency in parliamentary practices (e.g. secret ballots and the conciliation committees), as well as the significant degree of informality in the parliament around lobbying. We would hope that academic access is not compromised or impeded due to the parliamentary reforms, whilst at the same time increasing the transparency obligations of all the staff and MEPs working both within and without the European Parliament premises.

New or extended parliamentary powers and reforms may also bring about new analytical foci and affect the points of entry, actors and settings to be engaged with, as happened with the increasing powers of the European Parliament following the Lisbon Treaty reforms. We also saw with the onset of Covid-19, how we were obliged to turn the pandemic-related scientific and technical problems into research and academic opportunities. First, the technical and institutional access problems (travel restrictions and remote work modes) changed our means of data gathering as we conducted interviews online or via telephone.

We also experienced new layers to data collection due to the Covid-19 restrictions, which resulted in novel approaches and methodological contributions.

Secondly, Covid-19 restrictions have yielded a new research field on the democratic access, transparency, and the policy content of EU responses. Crises often exacerbate existing inequalities, and the Covid-19 pandemic has been no exception: inequalities based on gender, race and ethnicity, disability, sexual orientation, age and class have become more marked, and those already vulnerable even more so. In the vein of exploring the new policy areas that a parliament can have influence in, Elomäki and Kantola (2023) in an article on 'Feminist governance in the European Parliament: The political struggle over the inclusion of gender in the EU's Covid-19 response', looked at lessons learned from previous crises, and collaborations across political group lines in the current situation. Unexpected future developments or policy crises will undoubtedly provide ample material for further research along similar lines.

The relationship(s) between the executive and parliaments may also bring about changes in the focus for research. As we have seen at the EU level, subsequent Commission Presidents led efforts to make their own mark on EU policy processes and reforms in different fields. We experienced variance in the approaches to gender equality and economic and social policy, amongst other things, as different levels of priority were placed on them by Barroso, Juncker and von der Leyen in just the last 15 years. We have explored these in several publications (see for instance, Berthet, 2022a, 2022b; Elomäki, 2021; Elomäki & Ahrens, 2022; Elomäki & Gaweda, 2022) aiming to explore the changes, often in longitudinal or time—and context-specific ways. Looking forward, explorations of change in the institutional and behavioural processes as well as in policy-making will always remain core research foci for parliamentary studies.

Relatedly, future research could focus on the materialism of parliaments, involving not only their physical spaces (Verge, 2022), but also the socio-economic organisation and their embeddedness in the locations. In particular, anthropological literature has been good at pursuing this angle (Lewicki, 2016). For example, in the case of the European Parliament, its surrounding infrastructure could and should be examined, extending the research discussion to the relationship of EU institutions with Brussels and Strasbourg as locations. The power hierarchies, and how they play out in the spaces of Brussels and Strasbourg in relation to domestic populations, should also be examined. From an intersectional gendered point of view, issues such as childcare and child rearing infrastructures in Belgium or France; racist policing; and also the Strasbourg seat and its relationship with the constituencies could be prime bases for future research. Moreover, parliaments have large budgets, so studies of procurement contracts could be conducted to ensure that they are socially just. Furthermore, considering the massive contemporary global challenges, future parliaments should be expected to move towards greener and more sustainable solutions. Thus, the ways these transformations occur should also be an area of future enquiry.

We conclude with the wish that this guide will be of equal help to those who are exploring more established agendas, as well as researchers who are investigating new avenues of research. As beacons of democracy where anti-democratic and anti-gender forces play out, parliaments will certainly present more, rather than less, topics to research qualitatively.

References

Berry, J. M. (2002). Validity and reliability issues in elite interviewing. *Political Science & Politics, 35*(4), 679–682.

Berthet, V. (2022a). Norm under fire: Support for and opposition to the European Union's ratification of the Istanbul Convention in the European Parliament. *International Feminist Journal of Politics, 24*(5), 675–698.

Berthet, V. (2022b). United in crisis: Abortion politics in the European Parliament and political groups' disputes over EU values. *Journal of Common Market Studies, 60*(6), 1797–1814.

Beyers, J., Braun, C., Marshall, D., & De Bruycker, I. (2014). Let's talk! On the practice and method of interviewing policy experts. *Interest Groups & Advocacy, 3,* 174–187.

Crewe, E. (2021). *The anthropology of parliaments: Entanglements in democratic politics.* Taylor & Francis.

Elomäki, A. (2021). "It's a total no-no": The strategic silence about gender in the European Parliament's economic governance policies. *International Political Science Review, 0*(0). https://doi.org/10.1177/019251212097832

Elomäki, A., & Ahrens, P. (2022). Contested gender mainstreaming in the European Parliament: Political groups and committees as gatekeepers. *European Journal of Politics and Gender, 5*(3), 322–340.

Elomäki, A., & Gaweda, B. (2022). Looking for the 'Social' in the European semester: The ambiguous 'socialisation' of EU economic governance in the

European Parliament. *Journal of Contemporary European Research, 18*(1), 166–183.

Elomäki, A., & Kantola, J. (2023). Feminist governance in the European Parliament: The political struggle over the inclusion of gender in the EU's COVID-19 response. *Politics & Gender, 19*(2), 327–348.

Fitsilis, F., & Mikros, G. (Eds.) (2022). *Smart parliaments: Data-driven democracy.* European Liberal Forum. Retrieved 27 April 2023, from https://liberalforum.eu/wp-content/uploads/2022/11/Smart-Parliaments_Techno Politics-Vol.4.pdf

Fowler, J. H., Heaney, M. T., Nickerson, D. W., Padgett, J. F., & Sinclair, B. (2011). Causality in political networks. *American Politics Research, 39*(2), 437–480.

Lewicki, P. (2016). European bodies?: Class and gender dynamics among EU civil servants in Brussels. *Anthropological Journal of European Cultures, 25*(2), 116–138.

Saldana, J. (2021). Affective coding methods. In J. Saldana (Ed.), *The coding manual for qualitative researchers* (4th ed., pp. 105–110). SAGE Publishing.

Verge, T. (2022). Too few, too little: Parliaments' response to sexism and sexual harassment. *Parliamentary Affairs, 75*(1), 94–112.

Warasin, M., Kantola, J., Rolandsen Agustín, L., & Coughlan, C. (2020). Politicisation of gender equality in the European Parliament: Cohesion and inter-group coalitions in plenary and committees. In P. Ahrens & L. Rolandsen Agustin (Eds.), *Gendering the European Parliament: Structures, policies and practices* (pp. 141–158). Rowman and Littlefield, ECPR press.

Appendix A: Informed Consent

European Research Council

Established by the European Commission

Consent to Participate in a Research Study
University of Tampere, Finland
Title of the Study:
Gender, party politics and democracy in Europe:
A study of European Parliament's party groups

Principle
Investigator: _____   Affiliation: _____
Researcher: _____   Affiliation: _____

© The Editor(s) (if applicable) and The Author(s) 2023   139
V. Berthet et al., *Guide to Qualitative Research in Parliaments*,
https://doi.org/10.1007/978-3-031-39808-7

Thank you for agreeing to be [insert **interviewed/shadowed**] for the purposes of the research project: Gender, party politics and democracy in Europe: A study of European Parliament's party groups (EUGenDem), University of Tampere, Finland, and funded by the European Research Council Consolidator Grant (2018–2023).

We would kindly ask you to read this form and ask any questions that you may have before agreeing to be [insert interviewed/shadowed].

Purpose of the Study

The purpose of the study is to study European Parliament's political groups' practices and policies from a gender perspective. This means studying questions such as: which factors either advance and hinder women and men's political careers within the political groups.

Ultimately, this research may be presented as conference papers, or published academic books and journals.

Interview Procedures and Confidentiality

This interview will last from 30 minutes to 2 hours. It will be recorded with your permission and later transcribed. The interview data is fully confidential. We will guarantee your full anonymity. You will have the opportunity to see the citations we might later use in research. The interviews will be used only for the purposes of this research project. We will not include any information in any report we may publish that would make it possible to identify you.

The records of this study will be kept strictly confidential. Research records will be kept in a locked file, and all electronic information will be coded and secured using a password-protected file.

Benefits of the Study

The benefits of participation are for the society to better understand how the European Parliament's political groups potentially are shaped by gender relations. If these are unequal to any gender, they can be addressed as a result of this study.

Payment

Please note that there is no payment or reimbursement for this [insert interview/shadowing placement].

Right to Refuse or Withdraw

The decision to participate in this study is entirely up to you. You may refuse to take part in the study *at any time* without affecting your relationship with the investigators of this study. You have the right not to answer any single question, as well as to withdraw completely from the [insert interview/shadowing placement] at any point during the process; additionally, you have the right to request that the researcher not use any of [insert the interview material/ the material accessed through shadowing placement].

Right to Ask Questions and Report Concerns

You have the right to ask questions about this research study and to have those questions answered by us before, during or after the research. If you have any further questions about the study, at any time feel free to contact us, [insert contact details]. If you have any other concerns about your rights as a research participant that have not been answered by the investigators, you may contact [insert contact details].

Consent

Your signature below indicates that you have decided to volunteer as a research participant for this study, and that you have read and understood the information provided above. You will be given a signed and dated copy of this form to keep, along with any other printed materials deemed necessary by the study investigators.

Signature and Date

APPENDIX B: INFORMATION SHEET ABOUT THE PROJECT

European Research Council

Established by the European Commission

Information sheet about the Research Project
University of Tampere, Finland
Title of the Study:
**Gender, party politics and democracy in Europe:
A study of European Parliament's party groups**

Principle
Investigator: _____ Affiliation: _____
Researcher: _____ Affiliation: _____

© The Editor(s) (if applicable) and The Author(s) 2023
V. Berthet et al., *Guide to Qualitative Research in Parliaments*,
https://doi.org/10.1007/978-3-031-39808-7

Purpose of the Study

Gender, party politics and democracy in Europe: A study of European Parliament's party groups (EUGenDem) is an academic research project funded by the **European Research Council** (ERC) Consolidator Grant (2018–2023) and based at the University of Tampere, Finland.

The purpose of the study is to study European Parliament's political groups' practices and policies from a gender perspective. This means studying questions such as: which factors either advance and hinder women and men's political careers within the political groups.

Ultimately, this research may be presented as conference papers, or published academic books and journal articles.

Benefits of the Study

The benefits of the research are for the society to better understand how the European Parliament's political groups potentially are shaped by gender relations. If these are unequal to any gender, they can be addressed as a result of this study.

Data Collection

Our research data involves a lot of written public **documents** but we also conduct **interviews** in the parliament with MEPs, their assistants and EP's personnel. In addition, we undertake **participant observation** in public events and public meetings. We also undertake some participant observation in some closed meetings if we are given the permission. In these cases, everyone who participates in the meetings is informed beforehand. All the data that we collect is anonymised and no one can be recognised at any stage. All data is also stored securely. When making field notes during participant observation no personal data (such as names or nationalities) is recorded.

Right to Ask Questions and Report Concerns

You have the right to ask questions about this research study and to have those questions answered by us before, during or after the research. If you have any further questions about the study, at any time feel free to contact us, [insert contact details]. If you have any other concerns about your rights as a research participant that have not been answered by the investigators, you may contact [insert contact details].

Contact Details

[insert contact details].

For more information about the research project please visit our website: [insert website link].

INDEX

© The Editor(s) (if applicable) and The Author(s) 2023   147
V. Berthet et al., *Guide to Qualitative Research in Parliaments*,
https://doi.org/10.1007/978-3-031-39808-7

The manufacturer's authorised representative in the EU is Springer Nature Customer Service Centre GmbH, Europaplatz 3, 69115 Heidelberg, Germany. If you have any concerns regarding our products, please contact ProductSafety@springernature.com

Printed and bound by CPI Group (UK) Ltd, Croydon, CR0 4YY

24/04/2026

02096354-0001